TOGETHER
for
FESTIVALS

a resource anthology

CHURCH INFORMATION OFFICE
Church House, Dean's Yard, Westminster, SW1P 3NZ

ISBN 0 7151 0333 4

Published for the General Synod Board of Education 1975
Second reprint 1981

Printed in England by Bocardo & Church Army Press Ltd, Cowley, Oxford

CONTENTS

FOREWORD

Together means what its name implies. It is a shared enterprise in religious education—a magazine that has as contributors clergy, day school teachers, Sunday school teachers, parents . . . all who are concerned with religious education. It is published by the Church Information Office for the General Synod Board of Education, but *Together* is not a ' party ' magazine; it is ecumenical both in outlook and readership.

One of the queries most frequently addressed to its Editor concerns 'something new for Easter (or Ascension or whenever') while one of the most usual openings to contributors' letters is, ' This year we tried a different approach to Easter (or whenever) which the children greatly enjoyed, and we wondered if you would be interested. . . .'

Yes, we *are* interested, and we hope that you will be too. In this volume we would like to share some of these new approaches to the great festivals of the Christian Year, and also to highlights of the community's year such as Harvest and Guy Fawkes. You will find here songs and stories, plays, lesson courses, ideas for family services—all tried out in practice, most of them worked out after discussion with the children, and all trying to help children and parents alike, through the medium of their own experiences, towards a deeper understanding of these tremendous events which are at once solemn and joyful, incomprehensibly abstract and yet reassuringly concrete.

The only festival which you will *not* find here is Christmas. We needed another volume for that! Look out for *Together at Christmas (CIO)*. Nor will you find Advent in its traditional place at the beginning of this book; we feared that the casual reader might think we had produced *two* books on Christmas—so instead we begin with a different sort of beginning: ' A New Baby for Mother Church' on Mothering Sunday, and then we follow the year round until we end with Epiphany.

One last word. These are only ideas and examples. Don't treat them as sacred. They will be far better if you adapt them, alter them, make up your own service or play round the basic theme, as best suits your own group and circumstances. *Together* is, above all, a shared enterprise.

Pamela Egan
Editor, *Together*

MOTHER CHURCH HAS A NEW BABY

. . . and Alan Beck has an idea for a most unusual Mothering Sunday service!

When we had a baptism booked for Mothering Sunday, it seemed a marvellous opportunity to combine the usual Mothering Sunday Service with the christening. The parents readily agreed and provided the 'props' needed for the first part of the Service, which in outline went as follows:—

Mothering Sunday is all about 'mothers' and 'Mother Church'. What an exciting day when a wife becomes a mother and a new baby joins the family! So this day is exciting for Mother Church, for she is just about to have a baby! Exciting for us too, as we are going to help that baby to be born and to join her great big family. So we had better learn what happens when babies are born.

1. It is most important to have someone there to help, so as soon as the birth begins Dad goes to the 'phone and rings up the hospital, then hurries to get out the car and drive mother off to hospital.

2. As soon as baby is born a little label is immediately put on baby's wrist with the surname written on it so that there can be no mistake made. [*Here the actual hospital label that belonged to the baby to be baptised was produced and shown round.*]

3. Baby is bathed and dressed. [*Here the baby's bath and its first nightdress were shown.*]

4. Baby is put in a cot in a nursery with a light on so that even when it's dark he'll feel safe. [*Here a nursery light was shown.*]

5. Soon baby will need to be fed. [*Baby's bottle shown.*]

6. Later on he will begin to learn. [*Nursery ABC Book displayed.*]

7. People at the Clinic, or Mum's friend the Health Visitor, will call to check on progress. [*Someone from the local Clinic now stood up.*]

Now Mother Church is to have a new baby right here!

1. You and I are here to help.

2. Listen and you will hear the *Christian* name given. [*Baptism Certificate shown.*]

3. You will see baby being washed [*draw attention to the font*] and dressed. Actually, he is wearing his christening robe already, the white robe of the Christian. You will see an *invisible* robe put on, the sign of the cross.

4. Mother Church will light a light for baby. [*A candle, old-fashioned but reliable!*]

5. Soon baby will need Christian food [*a child's first Prayer Book shown.*]

6. And Christian training [*Bible story book shown.*]

7. And there are no less than three ' Health Visitors ' to help Mum and Dad to see that this new child of the Church grows up strong in the Faith. [*Godparents asked to stand up.*]

A hymn and the baptism followed, and proud mother showed her baby to the children as they left.

A FAMILY SERVICE FOR MOTHERING SUNDAY

This service was devised by David Bartlett and the children of his congregation

The theme of this Service was 'The Family' and was in three parts. First, our own family, with the emphasis on mothers: second, the Holy Family, especially Mary, the mother of Jesus: and third, the family of the Church.

The children in the Sunday schools had previously made small gifts for their mothers (mainly bookmarks made of sugar paper, cut with pinking shears and decorated with lace, ribbon, cut-out pictures of flowers, designs, etc. according to the children's abilities). These were placed in bundles on the altar before the service, and the teachers distributed them to their children at the appropriate time. A few extra gifts were made for children who were not at Sunday school to give to their mothers (and grand-mothers, if present).

These gifts were particularly appropriate as the primary children had recently been doing a course of lessons called 'Surprises', and the juniors 'Signs and Symbols'; and we explained the gifts as a Surprise for mother and as a Symbol of our appreciation for our mothers.

The junior children had also been asked to write down their thoughts about 'Mother', and what she meant to them. These thoughts were sorted out and arranged into the readings at the beginning of the Service. They also formed the basis for the words of the hymn 'Thank you'.

Introduction
Priest: God said: 'Honour your father and your mother, that your days may be long in the land which the Lord your God gives you.' As today is Mothering Sunday, we have come to Church for three main reasons: first . . .

8

1st reader: . . . to praise God and to thank him for the love and devotion of our parents, especially our mothers;

for all they do for us,

and for all that they mean to us;

and to thank him for all the happiness of our family life,

and for our homes where we feel secure and loved.

Priest: Secondly . . .

2nd reader: . . . to thank God for Mary, the mother of Jesus, blessed among women; for her example of loyalty and obedience to the will of God, by whose example of motherhood many women have been encouraged and inspired.

Priest: And thirdly . . .

3rd reader: . . . to thank God for our spiritual mother, the Church; whose family we joined when we were baptised; through whom we come to learn the Christian faith; and by whom our footsteps can be guided into the way of peace.

Hymn: ' For the beauty of the earth ' (or ' Now thank we all our God ').

Readings: 'Mothers'

Priest: First then we give thanks for our own mothers. A few weeks ago our Junior Sunday school children were asked to write down their thoughts about Mummy, and what she meant to them. These thoughts have been arranged to try to help us this afternoon in our thinking as we give thanks for our mothers. The younger members thought mainly of the obvious practical things which mothers do for us.

1st reader: Our mothers are kind and loving; they keep our homes nice and clean; they light the fire and have a lovely warm house for us to come home to, especially when it is very cold.

2nd reader: They tidy our bedrooms, and even put away our toys for us, and they make sure we have a nice warm bed to sleep in.

3rd reader: They do the shopping, and cook us nice hot meals; and they make nice cakes when we have friends in for tea.

1st reader: They buy our clothes and make dresses for us girls; and they wash our clothes for us, so that we look neat and tidy.

2nd reader: They give us our pocket-money every week, and buy us nice presents at Christmas and on our birthdays; and they feed our pets for us.

3rd reader: They look after us and take care of us; they nurse us when we are not well, and they bathe our cuts for us when we fall over and hurt ourselves.

All readers: And sometimes they let us stay up late.

Priest: The older children thought more of the less obvious, but equally necessary, things that mothers do and what they are:

1st reader: Our mothers help us with our work.

2nd reader: They keep us healthy.

3rd reader: They teach us manners, and they comfort us when we have worries.

1st reader: Our mothers are nice.

2nd reader: They are kind and loving.

3rd reader: They are sympathetic and unselfish—when they are in a good mood.

1st reader: Mummy to us means . . . home:

2nd reader:—happiness:

3rd reader:—comfort:

All readers:—love and security.

Priest: And finally here are the thoughts of five children, exactly as they were written down:

1st reader: My mother means to me a person who would comfort me, a person who will understand and help me to become a proper person.

2nd reader: My mother is helpful and kind. She loves me, and sometimes she gets angry.

3rd reader: My mum is very nice and I love her. I shall not want her to go away.

1st reader: My mother means to me like a shepherd who guides me; she is kind and understanding; she comforts me. But sometimes I do not like her because she does not understand: then she blows her top.

2nd reader: To me I think that my mum is a very helpful and sympathetic person, and she gives me a lot of love, which is all that matters.

Priest: Would all the children please say to their mothers:
'Thank you, Mummy, for being so loving and kind.'
[*Children repeat.*]

Will all the fathers please say to their wives:
'Thank you for caring so well for our family.'
[*Fathers repeat.*]

And will all the mothers please reply:
'And thank *you* for *your* help at home.'
[*Mothers repeat.*]

(*Note: many people commented on how personal and warm this last part made the Service*)

Blessing and Distribution of Gifts

Prayers of thanksgiving for family life, and for those without happy homes.

Hymn: 'Thank you'—tune as in 'Thank you for every new good morning' in *Youth Praise*, published by Falcon Books.

Thank you for our nice cheerful homes, Lord;
Thank you for fires so warm and bright;
Thank you for games and toys and for
    Our cosy beds at night.

Thank you for presents, treats and clothes, Lord
Thank you for all our drink and food;
Thank you for holidays and outings
    Which we find so good.

Thank you for mothers and for fathers;
Thank you for others far away;
Thank you for brothers and for sisters
    With whom we can play.

Thank you for all that mothers do, Lord;
Thank you for all the love they show;
Thank you for ways they soothe and cheer us
    When we're feeling low.

[*Adults only*]
Thank you for your great gift of children;
Thank you for all the joy they give;
Help us to demonstrate to them
    The way they ought to live.

[*All*]
Thank you for all we do together;
Thank you for joys of family life;
Bless us, and through your guidance keep us
    Safe from harm and strife.

Dramatic Presentation

'The boyhood of Jesus', Scene 1 from *A Man Called Jesus*, by J. B. Phillips (Fontana Books).

The Magnificat was sung in a modern version (as in *Faith, Folk and Nativity*, Galliard Press) by a small children's choir.

Prayer of thanks for the example of Mary, Mother of Jesus.

Hymn: 'Living Lord' (from *Thirty 20th Century Hymns*, Weinberger).

Address on 'The Church as a Family' (or 'The Church as our Mother').

Prayers for the Church and ourselves as members of it.

The Lord's Prayer.

Hymn: 'At the name of Jesus'.

Blessing.

'THANK YOU FOR MOTHERS'

A hymn for a Mothering Sunday service, in which all the children can take part, by Rosemary C. Stephens. The tune is 'Morning has Broken' (Songs of Praise, 30)

verse 1: Youngest children mime mothers with babies in arms, and then fathers working.

Father in heaven,
Thank you for mothers,
Loving and caring
All the day long;
Thank you for fathers,
Working to feed us,
Mothers and fathers
Loving and strong.

verse 2: 5s to 7s form Nativity tableau.

Thank you for Mary,
' Blest among women ';
She whom you chose
To mother your Son;
Pattern of goodness,
Trust and obedience,
Help us to love you
As she has done.

verse 3: Juniors bring forward a processional cross, and a Bible and chalice, which they raise at appropriate lines. In the last two lines they turn to face processional cross and join hands.

Guardian of truth,
The Church is our Mother:
Telling of Jesus,   (*Bible*)
Agent of grace,   (*Chalice*)
Filled with his Spirit,
Making us brothers,
Joining his people
In every place.

13

verse 4: Sung by congregation with the children.

Parents and children
Praise God together,
Praise for our homes
And all that he gives;
May we serve others
As serving Jesus,
Make every home
The place where he lives.

(Some of the words were difficult and had to be carefully explained while the children were learning them; this was mainly due to the limitations imposed by the tune, but we chose it because it was popular in ' pop ' circles and as a school hymn.)

GOING UP FOR THE PASSOVER

Jesus went up to Jerusalem for the Passover many times: first as an excited 12-year old with new adult duties, and lastly, the week before his death, to transform the feast for us with his 'new Covenant.' George H. Stevens looks at the story of this great Jewish feast

More than once we read in the gospels of Jesus ' going up to the city of Jerusalem ' for the Feast of the Passover—the first occasion being when he was twelve years old and the last occasion when he went up to suffer death on the Cross at Passover-time.

Washing pots and mending bridges
Passover must have been an exciting time for a Jewish boy in Palestine in the days of Jesus. For at least four weeks previously people would talk of little else. ' Spring-cleaning ' would be going on in the houses and housewives would be busy washing cups, pots and brass vessels (see St Mark 7. 4). New clothes would also have to be made for the festival, and as there were no professional tailors or dress-makers this would keep the girls and women busy! The Sanhedrin (the Jewish Council) would see that the roads were repaired and the bridges checked, in view of the number of pilgrims who would be travelling on them.

A glass drinking cup of the time of Jesus

Of course not everyone could go to the feast, but the Law required that every male Jew should ' appear before the Lord ' in Jerusalem at the three great Festivals of Pentecost, Tabernacles and, of course, Passover. In order to try to keep the commandment, Jews from other countries within reach of Palestine would come if at all possible and certainly all Palestinian Jews would make the effort unless they were unavoidably prevented by illness or some other urgent cause. We have seen that a Jewish boy became *Bar Mitzvah,* ' a son of the Commandment ', at 12 years old (13 in this country today) and from that age onwards had the privileges and duties of an adult Jew. This is probably why it is mentioned that Jesus went with his parents when he was twelve years old— possibly his first visit to Jerusalem since he was a baby.

Josephus, the Jewish historian, tells us that there were about two-and-a-half million Jews in Jerusalem for the Passover in A.D. 66. The number seems very large but they were used to sleeping out, covering themselves with their cloaks or outer garments, and every available space in the houses and inns could be used since no bedsteads were needed. At most they would use a pallet or portable mattress, such as that which Jesus told the sick man to take up and walk (St John 5. 8) and many would dispense even with this. Many pilgrims would camp outside Jerusalem and we read in the Talmud that the villagers of Bethphage and Bethany were especially renowned for their hospitality to pilgrims. It was in Bethany that Jesus and his disciples used to stay with Martha, Mary and Lazarus.

The Passover festival commemorates the deliverance of the children of Israel from slavery in Egypt under the hands of Moses. At the original Passover each family had to choose a lamb without blemish and sprinkle its blood on the doorpost of the house, so that the angel of destruction might pass over it (see Exodus 12. 1–14). For this reason, so long as the Temple stood in Jerusalem, families would bring their lambs to it to be sacrificed. It is estimated that in the days of our Lord over 250,000 lambs were offered at Passover time.

Passover is also the Feast of Unleavened Bread, since the children of Israel had to leave Egypt so hurriedly they had no time to leaven their loaves. Leaven (yeast) later came to be looked upon as a type of quickly-spreading evil, and on the eve of Passover (as still happens in Orthodox Jewish houses today) every nook and corner of every Jewish home would be searched by the head of the household to make sure no particle of leaven was left.

Firstborn with an appetite

The firstborn in every family would fast for the whole or part of the Day of Preparation as a token of his thanks that when the firstborn of Egypt were killed in the final plague, the firstborn Israelites were spared. This would mean that he would have a very good appetite for the Passover Feast when the next day began. Jesus was a real boy and a healthy young man and we can imagine him sharing in this experience with other eldest sons.

At last, then, on the evening of Nisan 14, the lambs having been killed in the afternoon, the family would gather around the Passover table to begin the feast as soon as the first star appeared to indicate that the next day, Nisan 15, had begun. (The Jewish day is always reckoned from sunset to sunrise, not from morning to midnight.)

The guests would keep their heads covered but would remove their shoes; if a servant was present he would wash their feet. We read how Jesus set a wonderful example of humility by washing his disciples' feet (St John 13. 4–50). They would then recline on the divans or cushions provided, and the Passover ritual would begin. Although Passover is a meal, it is also a service. Before the

A stone mill for grinding spices

meal the head of the household recites the *Haggadah*, the story of the first Passover and the deliverance of the Children of Israel from Egypt. At various points in the meal he says a solemn blessing over the wine to be drunk or the unleavened bread to be eaten. Much of the food eaten is symbolical: bitter herbs to remind those present of the bitter lot of their fathers in the land of Egypt; *haroseth*, a mixture of dates, pomegranates, almonds, apples, cinnamon and ginger, resembling the clay with which the Hebrew slaves had to make bricks in the land of Egypt. (This was probably the ' sop ' which our Lord gave to Judas.) There is, also of course, the unleavened bread, recalling 'the bread of affliction which your fathers ate in the land of Egypt'. One piece of unleavened bread is broken and distributed among the guests; another, known as the *Afiqumen*, is hidden in a napkin to be brought out (often discovered by one of the children) at the end of the meal. It was probably at this point that Jesus took the bread and broke it, giving it a new significance altogether when he said 'This is my body which is given for you.' Similarly in the Passover ritual there are four cups of wine to be drunk ceremonially, one of which is called 'the cup of blessing' (see St Paul's words in I Cor. 10. 16). This may well have been the cup which Our Lord described as his 'blood of the New Covenant'.

We can see from this that much of the Passover ceremonial has remained unchanged since the time of Christ. There is one great difference, however. Whereas in our Lord's day the lamb was the central item of the feast, today, as there is no Temple where the lambs can be sacrificed, there can be no lamb—although the shank-bone of a lamb is placed on the Passover table to remind everyone of what was once so important. Today the main dish will probably be fish or chicken, with no special symbolical meaning. Christians cannot help seeing significance in this, since they believe that Christ was himself the true Paschal lamb. In fact, in Matins on Easter Day instead of the Venite we sing St Paul's words 'Christ our passover is sacrificed for us, therefore let us keep the feast,' while the appointed Lesson is the Institution of the Passover from Exodus 12.

'Next year in Jerusalem!'

Passover looks forward as well as backward. Through the long centuries of exile, the Jews have said year by year 'At present we celebrate it here, but the next year we hope to celebrate it in the Land of Israel' and at the end of the meal have prayed 'Next year (grant us to be) in Jerusalem!' These hopes have now been literally fulfilled for the Israelis, but they have a deeper meaning. W. W. Simpson suggests the words mean much the same to the Jews as do those about building Jerusalem 'in England's green and pleasant land' to us. They look forward to the day when God will really dwell in the hearts of all men and the whole world will be Jerusalem, the city where God dwells.

So in the service of Holy Communion we say in the Prayer Book service 'until his coming again' and in Series II 'We look for the coming of his Kingdom'. Jews still say 'I believe that Messiah shall come and though he tarry I will wait for him'. Christians believe that Jesus *is* the Christ, the true Messiah, but like the Jews they long for the day when his Kingdom shall come in its fulness.

The children's festival

There is one final word to be said for those specially concerned with children. We often say that Christmas is the children's festival. The same thing is true of Passover for the Jews. The youngest present begins the ceremony by asking ' Why is this night different from all other nights?' Children usually find the *Afiqumen* and bring it to their father, perhaps with a reminder of something hoped for at their coming birthday! Children enjoy staying up later than usual, following the service in a beautifully illustrated picture-book, being allowed a sip of the wine and joining in the songs with which the feast ends. Children should always be made to feel at home in the House of God and especially, surely, at ' the great King's feast '.

Flat bread cooking over a charcoal fire

A MIME FOR MAUNDY THURSDAY: 1

First article in a series by Kathleen M. Hovey, describing how a group of a dozen 9–10 year olds explored the theme ' A Meal to Remember ', from ' Alive in God's World ', Second Series, Book 3 (CIO). They met in the church of their Cheshire village for an hour each week after the Parish Communion

The project began in January when, with Christmas parties a recent memory, there was no problem in compiling lists and charts of our favourite foods. Next, menus were planned for special occasions, each child keeping his a secret so that all had the fun of guessing the occasion. After so much about ourselves it was time to think of others and a menu for a Refugee's Christmas Dinner, ' A handful of rice ', displayed along with those planned for our own festivities, was a poignant reminder of those less fortunate than ourselves.

An idea that proved extremely popular with the girls was the meal we planned for a lonely person. After making tactful enquiries, the plans were carried out one cold, drizzling Sunday afternoon in late January and a house-bound old lady was entertained on what proved to be the day after her 70th birthday. One of the boys, not to be left out, contributed his pocket money to buy the milk.

The second phase of our work was concerned with the Jewish ' Meal to Remember '—the Feast of the Passover. We looked up the Biblical references of the Exodus and attempted to discover the symbolism of the Passover Feast. It was at this stage that the leaders (including the Vicar!) began to learn fascinating new facts from various sources. Wall charts were prepared from this information and the children were given question cards to answer, either from these charts or from Bible references. They were particularly

The Feast of the Passover

Look in the Old Testament. Find the Book of Exodus, Chapter 12.

What was the animal to be used for the meal? v 3

How was it to be cooked? vv 8, 9

What was to happen to any leftovers? v 10

What time of day was the feast to be? v 8

How were they to eat the meal? vv 11 and 12

Why did they have unleavened bread? Chap. 12 v 39

Copy out the verse (14) which commands the Jews to keep this feast.

Find a picture of the bitter herb hyssop. Draw it and label it.

How were the Jews to answer their children's question 'What mean ye by this service?' v 27

Copy out v 42 'It is a night . . . generations'.

A work card used in the project; another is given below

Preparation—the Women's Part

Before the Passover the women had a very busy time. They had to '*spring-clean*' *the house*, throwing away any leavened bread. This was to be the first month of the year and was the time for *new clothes*. They had to *bake the unleavened bread* and prepare special foods such as *haroseth*—a mixture of apples, wine and nuts. (This represented the mortar for the bricks.)

Find a picture of an eastern house. Look at it carefully, then draw or paint your own picture of the women spring cleaning.

Make out a list of ' jobs to be done ' before the Passover.

Describe how you would set the table that evening.

There was a lot to explore in the women's role

interested in the symbolism of the meal, especially the bowl of salt water to represent tears of sorrow, and the *haroseth* (a mixture of stewed apples, wine and nuts) which stood for the mortar for the bricks. The girls made lists of the jobs to be done by the women (the picture of an Eastern house interior, by E. A. Wood, which is full of detail, proved useful here) while the boys learned about the men's part.

Meals that Jesus shared

Meanwhile we thought together of the occasions when Jesus shared meals with his friends. (Good revision exercise, this—there are more than you might at first think!) We used the Nelson pictures by the Cockfosters Sisters to jog the children's minds when necessary, but it was encouraging to discover how many of the stories they could recall without help from us. This led naturally to our thinking together about Christ's Last Supper with his disciples and then on to our present Holy Communion Service.

It was as we discovered together the close links between the Jewish Passover customs and our own Communion liturgy that we found we wanted to share our knowledge. The dramatic possibilities of the theme had become increasingly apparent. As we were already in Lent, Maundy Thursday seemed to be an ideal date for our presentation. An evening Celebration was already planned and we were invited to present our mime as part of that Service.

A MIME FOR MAUNDY THURSDAY: 2

The mime itself

Setting: One large table in the centre of the acting area. A small table to one side. Near at hand three bench kneelers on which the boys will ' recline ' round the table.

Properties: A fair linen cloth; two candlesticks and candles; a goblet; a large round or oval dish; a dish containing stewed apples (to represent the *haroseth*): a large shank bone; a small bowl containing salt water; a dish of bitter herbs (we used parsley); cinnamon sticks if available; three pieces of unleavened bread or ' matzos ' (large-size water biscuits are a possible substitute, but it is better to use the authentic wafers).

Costumes: Simple tunics made from curtains. Head-dresses for the boys were rectangular pieces of material secured by a narrow scarf or cord. The girls made head-bands from gold coins (after the chocolate had been removed!) These secured their veils.

Part One

[*The Narrator stands to one side of the acting space. The girls enter, miming the spring cleaning, and the other tasks mentioned. As the Narrator proceeds, they set the table, put the benches in position and place all the food, except the bread and wine, on the side table.*]

Narrator: The days before the Passover were busy ones for the Jewish housewife. She cleaned her home from top to bottom, being particularly careful to ensure that no leavened bread was left in the house. She also had to bake the unleavened bread and prepare other special foods.

On the evening of the Passover the men went to a service at the synagogue. While they were away she set the table using her finest white cloth. On this were placed two candlesticks, a large oval or round dish containing three pieces of unleavened bread, a large wine-glass or goblet and a bowl of salt water to represent the tears of affliction in the land of bondage. There was also a dish of bitter herbs to remind them

23

of the bitterness of slavery and some *haroseth* (a mixture of stewed apples, wine and nuts) to represent the clay or mortar for the bricks. A shank bone was used in place of the Paschal Lamb, cinnamon sticks took the place of straw.

Part Two

[The women wait at the side. The men return from the synagogue and take their places at table. They ' kneel up ' on the benches so that they are not hidden from the congregation.]

Narrator: The men return from their evening prayers and take their places at the table. The seat of honour at the head of the table is taken by the eldest man, who is called the President of the Feast.

[The President rises and is given the cup of wine.]

President: Blessed art Thou, O Lord Our God, King of the Universe, Creator of the fruit of the vine.

All: Amen.

[The cup is passed round all the guests. Each has a sip of the ' wine '.]

Narrator: The *haroseth,* representing the clay for the bricks, is brought to the table. *[One of the girls brings it]* All dip in the same dish. *[The dish is passed round]* The rest of the meal is served *[by the girls].*

Then the youngest boy asks several questions of the President. *[The Haggadah contains four questions. We limited them to the first two].*

Youngest boy: Why is this night different from all other nights? For on all other nights we may eat either leavened or unleavened bread, but on this night only leavened.

On all other nights we may eat other kinds of herbs, but on this night only bitter herbs.

Narrator: The President then explains the symbolism of the meal. First he lifts the dish to display the bread.

President: This is the bread of sorrow that our fathers ate in the Land of Egypt. We eat unleavened bread on this night because our fathers were delivered out of Egypt in such haste that there was no time for them to wait until their dough was leavened.

[Lifts bitter herbs] We eat bitter herbs on this night because the Egyptians made bitter the life of our fathers with hard service in Egypt.

24

[*Picks up the lamb*] We eat the Paschal or Passover Lamb on this night because God in his mercy passed over the houses of our fathers in Egypt, but destroyed the firstborn of the Egyptians.
[*At this point the Lay Reader reads the Old Testament Lesson— the story of the first Passover*].

Narrator: Now the President takes the unleavened bread and blesses it.

President: Blessed art Thou, O Lord Our God, King of all the World, who causes bread to come forth from the earth.

All: Amen. [*The President breaks off a piece for each person and gives it to them in turn*].

President: Speak praises to God, to whom belongs what we have eaten.

All: Praised be our God for the food we have eaten.
[*The Gospel (the story of Maundy Thursday) is then read, followed by the Creed. The boys then leave the scene, taking their places in the front pews. The girls, meanwhile, clear the tables, leaving only the candlesticks, the unleavened bread and the goblet, which are used later in the service at the Communion.*]

Producing the Mime

Too much rehearsing tends to spoil the spontaneity required in presenting a mime. By including the stage directions in the narrative it was possible to manage with about four 'practices'. These included two morning sessions on the Monday and Tuesday of Holy Week, with the dress rehearsal on the Wednesday evening. The narrative and action developed as we tried out new ideas, the final script being the one which suited our conditions best. It would, of course, be possible to adapt it for use in other buildings.

Its beauty was in its simplicity and it gained immensely from the fact that we were privileged to present it as part of the Communion service.

A MIME FOR MAUNDY THURSDAY: 3

Kathleen M. Hovey describes how the Passover mime fitted into the Communion service

Note: The church in which this service took place was fortunate in having an open space in front of the chancel steps, sufficiently large to enable a temporary altar to be erected in the middle while still leaving plenty of room for movement all round and also for the communicants to kneel on three sides. At the beginning of the service the altar was bare apart from the candlesticks, and represented the table used for the Passover meal.

Before the service began one of the teachers explained to the congregation what the children had been doing in recent weeks— i.e. favourite meals, refugee menu, visit to old lady, our Lord's meals with his friends and, especially, the Last Supper. They were then told that the children would enact a Passover meal in mime against the background of a Series II Holy Communion Service.

The opening hymn was 'Let us with a gladsome mind', (AMR 377). This was chosen because, in a village church with limited musical resources, it was one of the most appropriate of those hymns which are paraphrases of the psalms. More ambitious parishes might consider beginning with one of the actual Passover psalms (114–118). Another alternative is for everyone to listen to a recording of the Passover Psalm sung by Owen Brannigan and a male voice choir (Grail Records No. GR 3–4).

The congregation then sat while the girls mimed the women's part of the Passover Preparations to a commentary from the teacher (see article 2 of this series).

The Vicar and congregation next said together the Collect for Purity, followed by the Vicar saying the Maundy Thursday collects. The mime then continued with the men's part, beginning with their return from evening worship at the synagogue. One of the boys acted as President and spoke where appropriate. The only other speaking part was that of the youngest child asking ' What mean ye by this Service ? ' (See Exodus 12. 25–27).

26

The unleavened bread

After the explanation of the symbolism of the Paschal Lamb, the Lay Reader read, for the Epistle, Exodus 12. 1–11. Note that in the NEB and some other versions, some of the verses may be omitted without disturbing the essential part of the narrative.

The mime then concluded with the eating of the unleavened bread. At this point the congregation stood while the Vicar read, for the Gospel, St Matthew's account of our Lord's actions, Matthew 26. 26–30.

The service continued with Holy Communion Series II from the Creed onwards, except that the Intercession took the following form:

Lay Reader: Let us pray for the whole Church of God in Christ Jesus and for all men according to their needs.

1st Child: Let us pray for Christians everywhere as they prepare to celebrate the death and resurrection of the Lord Jesus.

Reader: Lord in thy mercy

All: Hear our prayer.

2nd Child: Let us pray for all who receive the Holy Communion and for those who are preparing for Confirmation:

Reader: Lord in thy mercy . . . .

3rd Child: Let us pray for the Jewish people and for all who are not Christians or who have turned away from the Christian Faith:

4th Child: Let us pray for all who suffer because they believe in Jesus.

5th Child: Let us pray for those who have little or no food to eat, especially in those countries where there is famine or war.

6th Child: Let us pray for the work of Christian Aid and for all those organisations who are trying to help those in need:

The Reader then took up the concluding words of the Series II intercession ' Grant these our prayers '. The Offertory hymn was ' Bread of Heaven ', AMR 411. (Part One of ' Now my tongue the mystery telling,' AMR 383, is also particularly suitable.) During this hymn the same table which the boys had used for their mime was prepared for the Eucharist and the candles were lit. On this occasion unleavened bread was used for the Communion of the people. The post Communion hymn was ' The King of Love my Shepherd is ' (AMR 197), another paraphrase link with Jewish worship.

At the conclusion of the service tea and biscuits were served to the members of the congregation in the south transept of the church. The children's work in connection with the course was on display in this transept.

THE SPECIAL MEAL

A simple Holy Week service used by children of St Mark's, Bromley, Kent, C.E. Primary School

In the previous weeks the children had been learning about the giving of the manna in the wilderness; the feeding of the five thousand; and The Last Supper.

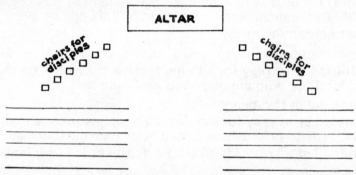

In church a free-standing altar was placed at the entrance to the chancel with an arc of chairs on each side of it for the ' disciples '. The service was conducted by a priest wearing alb, amice and stole. After an opening prayer the priest, standing *in front* of the altar, spoke to the congregation:

Priest: This week has a special name. What is it? That's right, Holy Week, because some of the most wonderful events that have ever happened took place in it.

Many of those events were both sad and bad, but there were also a few happy moments. This morning we are going to think about one of those happy occasions, which happened on the evening before Jesus died.

That day has a special name. Do you know what it is? Maundy Thursday. On that day Jesus ate his last meal with his friends.

There were three reasons why he did this. The Last Supper was intended to be:

A farewell meal. At it Jesus said ' Goodbye ' to his friends;

A memorial—something by which Jesus could be remembered. He asked his friends to go on doing this in remembrance of him.

A way of keeping his promise to feed the world with his own Body and Blood.

This last meal was held in the guest room of a friend's house. In that room there would have been a table shaped like a horseshoe, and Jesus and his friends would have sat round the outside of that table.

Jesus would have been wearing clothes a bit like those that I am wearing now. So as we go through the service, try to imagine that it is Jesus who is saying the words and doing the actions; forget that you are in.........and imagine you are in Jerusalem on the first Maundy Thursday.

[*The priest then went behind the altar and said*]:

Priest: The day before Jesus died, he sent two of his disciples into Jerusalem and told them to go to a certain house where he had previously arranged that he would have his last meal with his friends before he left them.

He told these two disciples that they would be shown a furnished room upstairs which contained everything necessary for the meal. They were to make the final preparations.

I want you to imagine that this church is that upper room. Here is the table and there are the seats for Jesus' friends. Instead of leaving all the preparations to just two of them, they are all going to do something to lay the table for this special meal.

First, the table is covered with a fine white cloth. [*Two 'disciples' brought up an altar cloth on a roller and laid it on the table*].

Then, because the meal will be eaten in the evening, two lighted candles are placed upon the table. [*Two more 'disciples' brought up candlesticks and placed them on the corners of the table. The candles had been previously lit.*]

Next, a cushion is put near the place where Jesus would have sat [*brought by another 'disciple'*] and the book containing the prayers is laid upon it.

Now the plate is brought for the bread [*Before laying this on the altar, the child turned and faced the congregation, showing them the paten*] and the cup for the wine [*also held up to be seen before being placed in position*].

29

Then a simple small loaf of bread, such as was used by everyone every day, is set in the centre of the table.

Lastly, two disciples bring a bottle of wine and a bottle of water. [*These also were shown to the children before being placed on the table.*]

Now all is ready for the Last Supper.

We know that one thing which Jesus and his disciples did was to sing hymns, which were probably psalms. So we are going to sing a modern version of the best-known and most loved of all the psalms, the 23rd. [*Use either 'The King of Love', or 'Crimond', but not 'The God of love my shepherd is', because it has no reference to a meal being prepared.*]

Reading: Exodus 16, vv. 2, 3, 4, 13b, 14, 15 (*in modern translation*) St John 6, vv. 30–33 and 48–51.

Hymn: 'Hands of Jesus' (from BBC Supplement).

Reading: I Corinthians 11, 23b–26.

Priest: Now I am going to say a prayer which tells us two things about this week. First, that Jesus died on the Cross so that when we leave this world we might go to live with him in heaven. Secondly, you will hear what happened at the Last Supper.

As I say the words that Jesus said, I shall break the bread as he did and bless the wine as he did. You must especially think of Jesus doing this through me, because after this prayer of blessing the bread and wine are still bread and wine, but they have also become in a special way his Body and his Blood and they are very holy things to be treated with great reverence.

The Prayer of Consecration.

Priest: Now we shall all say the prayer which Jesus himself taught us. I want you to think particularly about the words, 'Give us this day our daily bread'. This is a different kind of bread. It is food for our souls.

The Lord's Prayer.

Communion of Priest and People.

Priest: When someone gives us anything, it is very important that we remember to say 'Thank you' for it. This is good manners. It also shows how truly grateful we are to the person who gave us the gift. We are going to say 'Thank you' to God by singing our last hymn: 'Alleluia, sing to Jesus'.

Prayer 35 from Series 2 Holy Communion service.

The Blessing.

UNTIL HE COMES
A Passiontide play by Alan Beck

Every time you eat this bread and drink this cup, you proclaim the death of the Lord, until he comes. (I *Cor. 11. 26*)

Priest/Jesus	in full vestments, if worn.
Deacon/John	in alb and amice, if worn.
Sub-Deacon/Peter	as above.
Server/Judas	as above.
9 other Servers/Rest of the Twelve	as above.
Sacristan/Man with pitcher	in Eastern dress.
Church decorator/Wife of above	as above.
Centurion	in Roman soldier's uniform.
Soldiers	as above.
Three young men	in Eastern dress.
Five young girls	as above.
Evangelist	in cassock, surplice and scarf.
Preacher	as above.

Readings are taken from the *New English Bible.*

Introduction
Preacher goes to pulpit, Evangelist to Lectern. [*Both have the full script and a shaded light so that they can follow and could probably prompt if necessary.*] *Soft spotlight on Preacher.*

Preacher: Our play has two themes. One is the Holy Communion Service. The other, the events of the Passion which happened once in time for all time.

These two themes intermingle, for the Holy Communion Service itself is a re-enacting of the Passion as we, today, enter into Christ's death and share in his risen life.

Our story is set in Jerusalem at Passover-time. The city is full of pilgrims from all over Palestine. The mood is that of a religious festival and a national holiday. Yet there is also a brooding atmosphere of crisis. Soldiers are everywhere on watch. All feel the tension. Young people try to shrug it off by behaving with exaggerated jollity.

Jerusalem has many narrow streets, of which the nave of our church can represent one running to the well—one of the few open spaces where a crowd can gather. All the womenfolk of Jerusalem have to come here for water for their homes. We find them about their business, watched, no doubt, by young men.

Scene 1   Well at Jerusalem

[*Light fades from Preacher and area round font lit brightly.*]

Characters: 3 young men
5 girls with water pots
Centurion with spear
One or two other soldiers
Man with pitcher
Peter
John

Scene begins with hymn ' Once, only once, and once for all '.

[*Peter and John are up from the country and so the North-Country ' love ' has been used. The cast might suggest a more colloquial word.*

As lights come up, girls discovered round font gossiping while filling their water pots. Boys are perched on backs of seats or pews watching the girls. They discuss in mime which is the most attractive. Girls give sly looks and giggles. Soldiers stand, bored, in the background.]

Evangelist: *Reads* Luke 22. 7–10. (NB Stress ' a *man* will meet you '). [*Peter and John enter by West door.*]

Peter: Give us a drink, lass—thanks.
[*Sips from bowl and passes to John.*]

John: [*sips*] Thank you, love. [*Returns bowl to girl.*

She gives little curtsey, turns and titters with the others.]

Girl: [*Confides to rest*] Did you hear him call me love? I think he's rather nice!

[*Peter and John go discreetly to Library corner and sit conversing in dumb show of a business transaction, but keeping eye on well.*

First girl now shoulders pot with some hip-swinging and giving glances to the boys.

They give wolf whistle and as she moves off slowly up nave. First boy peels off perch and tries to make off with girl. She puts her nose in air and gives him cold shoulder. He goes back to perch, a bit crestfallen. Mutters ' Women ' to the other boys. She looks back to see effect on boys and sees Pitcher Man—turns, stares and comes back.

Enter (from porch) Pitcher Man. The others drop back and stare.]

Crowd: A man! Did you ever! What's he think he's doing?
[*He begins to fill his pot. One of the girls sniggers behind her hand.*]

1st Boy: Hey, Mister, where's your old woman? Gone off and left you? [*All snigger*].

2nd Boy: (*to neighbour*) Cor, look at him blushing—I don't reckon he's married. Don't think much of him for a man.
[*to man*] Hey, what about your duty to the nation? Israel expects every man to do his duty and raise sons of Israel.
[*He flexes masculine muscles*].

1st Boy: Roll on the day when I get a chance to do my duty and raise a few sons!
[*Winks at girl-friend. First girl giggles*].
Up the Sons of Israel!

All: Up the Sons of Israel!

Centurion: Now just you be a bit careful, you young Sons of Israel! We don't want any trouble these next few days over the Festival and I'll see there's peace and quiet on my beat, so you'd better get along.
[*They give him a surly look.*
Pitcher-bearer now sets pitcher on shoulder, trying to be indifferent to everything going on around him. As he starts to move up the nave, the girls shoulder pots and cut in front of him. They spin and turn to see how he is getting on. Boys join in with imaginary pots, imitating the girls.
Soldiers laugh.
Boys and girls move up nave. Peter and John pretend business concluded and follow at short distance.]

Evangelist: Jesus said, ' Anyone who wishes to be a follower of mine must leave *self* behind; he must take up his cross and come with me '.
[*All exit (except Preacher and Evangelist who stay in their places throughout) and lights faded out.*]

Scene 2   **The Holy Communion preparation/The Upper Room, Thursday afternoon.**
[*The scene takes place on a platform at the chancel step. Large standard candlesticks to left and right of stage.*
Lighting: suggest a browny-yellow light to be used throughout to indicate the upper room.]

Evangelist: Reads Luke 22. 11–12

[*A hymn is sung quietly during the scene.*
Enter Man with his pitcher. He sets it down. Wife enters and they move a small Nave altar from the side to centre stage. They get and put on a large heavy table-cloth or frontal.
Enter Peter with altar cloth and John with large bowl and towel.
Peter and John put cloth on altar then fetch chalice and paten and put them in place.
Man fetches wafers and wine cruet.
Woman gets flowers and puts on pedestal by pulpit.
Man gets small bowls as if containing herbs and tit-bits.
All arrange stools in a semi-circle with altar at centre, facing congregation.
All check everything, admire, bow to each other and exit.
Man returns and lights the two standard candles, exits.
Lights fade out and on again to indicate passage of time. As lights come up, next scene follows straight on.]

Scene 3   The Introit/The upper room, evening.

Evangelist: In the evening, he came to the house with the Twelve.
[*All sing a hymn (equals Introit) e.g. ' Take up thy cross '.*
Eucharistic procession enters from West Door, passes up Nave and if possible via a side route so that it can come down chancel and so on to the platform. If there are chancel gates, these can be shut behind the last person. Amices worn on the head until they pass through the gate and ' enter the upper room '.
Procession: Crucifier (one of disciples), Candle bearers (2), the rest of the Twelve, Priest/Jesus.
All take their places round the table facing the congregation, the two candles are set down on the altar and the processional cross put away. They remain standing.]

John: Master, will you bless our food and fellowship together?

Priest: Almighty God, to whom all hearts are open, all desires known, and from whom no secrets are hid; cleanse the thoughts of our hearts by the inspiration of your Holy Spirit, that we may perfectly love you, and worthily magnify your holy name.
[*All sit. Priest passes bowl to Peter (left), John (right) and all pass bowls to each other.*]

Evangelist: Then a jealous dispute broke out: who among them should rank highest?
[*The Twelve point and look at each other. Peter makes boxer's fists-up sign. John waves his hands across his face. Judas chokes, rest laugh.*
Jesus rises quietly and sadly, removes chasuble, puts towel round himself and begins to wash the feet of the disciples.]

Evangelist: Reads John 13. 2–11.
[*Choir sings ' Kyrie ' quietly during feet-washing.*
When Jesus has resumed his seat:]

Evangelist: Then Jesus said 'In truth, in very truth I tell you, one of *you* is going to betray me.'
[*All tumble back in confusion, pointing now to each other in panic (is it you)?, and then in horror to themselves (is it I?).*
Mime continues, while:]

Evangelist: Reads John 13. 23–30.
[*After Judas receives the sop, he exits through the chancel gates, shuts them quickly and exits via side route to go stealthily but hurriedly down nave. As he leaves:*]

Evangelist: Reads John 13. 31–32.
[*Creed begins quietly. Lights dim out on continuing meal. Cast stay where they are.*]

Sub-scene

[*The High Priest's House. Can be at the West door or perhaps where the Collection is normally counted. A dim light draws attention to action, very little of which can actually be seen—only shadows thrown on wall. Creed continues softly throughout, as contrast between faith and betrayal.*]

Preacher: With our lips we make our profession of faith in our Creed, but we know that in our lives we are often faithless to our Lord and Master. Is it I? Yes, every one of us is Judas the traitor. Whenever we should be giving but are taking. Whenever we forget his will because we are intent on our wishes. Whenever we want to be in control, and do things *our* way, then we are not worthy to sit at table and sup with Jesus. Is it I? Lord, we are not worthy so much as to gather up the crumbs under your table!
[*After pause, coins drop into bowl one at a time. Counted in hoarse whisper, at first by Judas only, then others, e.g. soldiers, add their whispers, growing in brutality to triumphant' Thirty!'. Coins poured into large bag. 'Ahh!' after rush of coins. Lights extinguished. Lights come up on Last Supper again.*]

The Offertory/The Last Supper continued

Preacher: Following the customs of the Eastern formal meal, it was now the time for the guest next to the person presiding at the meal to hand him the cup and ask him to bless it. And so in our remembrance of this last supper, in *our* family meal with our Master, we give him our gifts of bread and wine and ask him to bless them.

[*John gets up, goes to side table, takes the cup (round to front and presents it across the table). All kneel at table (upright). Jesus stands and makes the sign of the Cross—passes cup round.*]

Preacher: [*as cup is passed round*] Jesus gave to bread and wine a new meaning. He made them stand for his body and blood which he would soon give on the cross. All share this bread and cup, for all must share this death (though for us it is a death to self and sin) if we would share in the life of the eternal Christ —life set free by death.

[*All put amices over heads, James and John take candles, open gates, lead all into chancel, round and down by Lady Chapel, where all wait. Sacristan and wife remove supper things to side and extinguish candles. Stage is cleared, if possible in darkness.*]

Scene 4   The Intercession/Gethsemane

[*Cold blue light to represent moonlight. Disciples with Peter, James, John first, enter from side and move onto platform. Jesus passes through them into chancel. Disciples kneel, except Peter, James and John who remain standing. Peter and John hold candles. Jesus raises hands in prayer.*]

Preacher: Christ led his disciples to his favourite place of prayer, the Garden of Gethsemane, and he asked them to pray with him. He prayed that he might have strength to fulfil the Father's will, he prayed for his disciples, that they might work together in such peace and unity that the great mission for which he had called them and trained them might go forward unhindered. He prayed for the needs of all men, their real need—*our* real need, that evil might be overcome and God's Holy Will be done. We share this prayer as we pray for the whole Church of God, for its peace and unity and for the needs of all men, that God's Holy Will may be done.

[*Disciples sink to sleep*].

Preacher: But we, like the disciples, grow weary in prayer, our thoughts wander, and we are soon asleep.

[*Peter, James and John have sunk to knees and leaning on heels. Jesus rouses them*].

Preacher: Christ would rouse us to greater effort in prayer.

[*Peter, James and John slowly lie down, and extinguish candles. Jesus now kneels.*

A chalice, prominently placed on the high altar, is now lit with a soft blue local light and other light is slowly dimmed out.]

Evangelist: Jesus knelt down and began to pray 'Father, if it be thy will, take this cup away from me. Yet not my will but thine be done '.

And now there appeared to him an angel from heaven bringing him strength, and in anguish of spirit he prayed the more urgently; and his sweat was like drops of blood falling to the ground.

[*A suitable hymn may be sung. As hymn ends, light on cup fades and original blue lighting is brought on.*]

Preacher: Christ comes to his disciples once more and with outstretched arms he rouses them to follow him along the holy path of sacrifice. The priest bids us 'Lift up our hearts' and draw near to the climax of our act of remembrance as we recall the death of Jesus once, for all, on Calvary.

[*Jesus turns and approaches disciples, raises Peter and John who raise those next to them. So all are roused into a kneeling ring round Jesus. As the light on the chalice goes out. Judas creeps slowly up the nave, followed by as many soldiers as possible. One of them has a shielded lantern.*]

Jesus [*as he rouses the disciples*]: The Lord be with you.

Disciples: And also with you.

Jesus: Lift up your hearts.

Disciples: We lift them to the Lord.

[*The disciples move a little nearer, looking up to Jesus. Judas has now reached the edge of the circle and he goes crouching forward through them, as if to kiss Jesus.*

Jesus shrinks back, the soldiers become evident, and the disciples spring to their feet with the word 'Judas', which turns into a hiss of hatred. Judas falls back ashamed. Jesus' hands are still stretched out. He does not move. The soldiers hesitate for a moment, twist his hands behind his back, then grab the ends of his girdle and bind them round his hands.]

Disciples fall back right and left so that action can be seen, and adopt agonised attitudes as if turned to statues in the moment of grasping swords, lashing out, etc.

A soldier now goes to the front, exposes the lantern and holds it aloft. Soldiers fall in behind and march, almost marking time on the spot to make it seem further, taking Jesus up chancel (to clergy vestry if suitably placed.) The lantern is left just inside the open door to allow splash of light to spill into the church.

As soon as they have gone, the spell on the disciples breaks. Judas bolts for his life down the nave, going as fast as he dare in the dim light. The others blunder almost as if drunk, panting heavily, and crashing against the pews as they go. This should be made eerie and frightening.]

Scene 5   General Confession/Near the torture chamber
[Lighting—blue moonlight.]

Preacher: Every time we sin we betray Christ, every time we profess that we love Him but do not lovingly serve him in our neighbour, we give him a ' Judas ' kiss.

Every time we come to the Holy Communion unprepared, with our heart unexamined, as isolated individuals out of touch with those around us in church or about our home or around us at work; when we come with no real desire to be what God wants us to be, to do what he would have us do; then we are as useless as those sleeping disciples who fled the scene and were absent when Christ drained the cup of his passion for their sakes and for ours.

[Sounds of whipping come through the open vestry door. Perhaps a shadow could be cast on a wall of a whip rising and falling.

Preacher leads the saying of the Confession. Selected people in the congregation, possibly at the pew-ends, join in quietly.

As the confession ends, the Evangelist may read the comfortable words. The door to vestry is slowly shut and whipping ends. All lights extinguished.]

Scene 6   Consecration/Calvary
[Where the East Window or reredos consists of a crucifixion scene this should be used. Otherwise something must be improvised. If East Window is used, it should be illumined from outside by powerful spotlight.

After a pause in silence and total darkness; spotlight on East Window or crucifixion is brought slowly on to full. Centurion is discovered at the Communion rail looking up.
Either the Preacher and Evangelist together, or the disciples from the back of the church, or both, say slowly and quietly]:

For our salvation he was obedient even to death on the cross. By his death he has destroyed death, and by his rising again he has restored to us everlasting life. . . .
We break this bread to share in the body of Christ.

[Choir sings softly ' O Lamb of God. . . .'
The light slowly fades. As it fades the Centurion says boldly and with awe]:

Centurion: Truly, this was the Son of God. . . .
Thy Kingdom come!

[Blackout, exit centurion. During darkness, Preacher and Evangelist say slowly and quietly]:

As our Saviour has taught us, so we pray, ' Our Father . . . etc.'

Scene 7   Communion/Upper Room, Sunday

[Lighting for the upper room. Nave altar and standard candles in place on platform. (The scene has been set while the Lord's Prayer was being said.) As the lights come up]:

Preacher: Draw near with faith: receive the Body of our Lord Jesus Christ which he gave for you, and his Blood, which he shed for you. Remember, that he died for you, and feed on him in your hearts by faith with thanksgiving.

[Verger and wife reset the upper room, putting chalice and candles on the table. They light standard candles and exit. While they do this]:

Evangelist: Late that Sunday evening, the disciples were met together again in the upper room, behind locked doors for fear of the Jews.

[Disciples creep up the nave in ones and twos furtively. They come into the upper room as before, the last one shutting the door and checking that it is safely locked, the others watching him. They now relax a little and slump round the table. Jesus' place is left empty. No-one ventures to start the meal. At last John rises and lights the two table candles, and as he does so, Jesus enters unnoticed.]

39

Jesus [*calmly, with outstretched hands*]: Peace be with you. [*Gold spotlight rises in brightness on him.*

Disciples tumble about in confusion and joy, then adopt kneeling position as Jesus takes chalice and raises it as for the Elevation. Holds it high while the disciples say: ' Blessed is he who comes in the name of the Lord '.

Disciples form a semi-circle as if to receive Communion and all the cast can crowd in and kneel, though soldiers will not be wearing helmets. Those who have assisted in the congregation can also come forward and kneel, so that there is a great crowd to receive lighted tapers. Producer and stage hands, also join crowd.]

Choir: sing hymn ' Bread of Heaven '.

[*Priest lights small candle or taper from the altar and all produce tapers. Jesus lights nearest ones and these pass on the light until all are holding high their lighted taper.*

As hymn ends, all turn and process down nave, Priest going last, preceded by servers. As they process, all say boldly: Almighty God, we thank you for feeding us. . . .

Conclude with a congregational hymn, all lights coming up as procession leaves church by west door.]

THREE HOURS WITH THE CHILDREN

was a prospect of some alarm to the teachers in a Norfolk group of parishes—but that was before it all happened!

One of the highlights of a Training Day held for diocesan clergy and voluntary teachers in Norwich was a roomful of activities relating to a Good Friday Three Hours' service for children, held by a group of five village parishes. A tape-recording of parts of the service helped us to share the children's absorption, but easily the most impressive 'exhibit' was the enthusiasm of the helpers involved and their conviction that this demanding undertaking had been more than worthwhile.

The Rev. Alan Boar, vicar of the five parishes, spoke to us at the opening, and I later talked to him and to his helpers, who were on hand all day to demonstrate the handicrafts and other activities which had occupied the children. He told me that his original request to the Diocesan Adviser, Miss Marjorie Parry—made months before the actual event—was for a short service on much more traditional lines; when she suggested a full 'Three Hours' the reaction of everyone was one of actual horror. 'What on earth can we do with a crowd of young children for all that time?' they said. Mr Boar added, 'When Miss Parry told us that when the actual day came we would wish for *more* time, we frankly couldn't believe her . . . but that was before it happened!'

A band of 12 willing helpers was collected, each one ready to give up one evening a week during Lent to planning and preparation. Team and Adviser met regularly to discuss every detail necessary—possible activities, the form of worship, apparatus needed, the share-out of responsibilities. Publicity was vital and important. A letter was sent to every parent within the five parishes, describing the project and asking them to return a questionnaire listing the child's age, name, address and need (or not) for transport—an important point in so scattered a community. They were also asked to supply a packed lunch—squash to be provided by the organisers. 'We found it essential,' said Mr Boar, 'to collect the lunches as the children came in and label each one with its owner's name. Seventy children finally arrived, and without this precaution there could have been chaos.' On the day the children were divided into two age groups, under-7s and over-7s. Each child was given to take home a duplicated copy of the programme, folded and stapled into a booklet with cover, and containing the words of all the prayers and hymns. The service began at 12.15 p.m. with worship. The hymn ' What do I see as I gaze down the road?' from 27 *Twentieth Century Hymns* (published by Weinberger) had been chosen as the ' theme-song ', and the music of this was used to call the children together at the start of each period of worship.

The first period consisted of a short, very simply introductory talk, two prayers and ' Ride on, ride on in majesty ', after which the children dispersed to the various activities which will be described later. The second period, at 12.45 p.m., began to tell the story of the Cross from the viewpoint of the witnesses—first, St Peter. An existing set of figures was used, as a visual aid, to which others had been cleverly added for this service by a parishioner who worked in advertising. They were large, freestanding wooden cut-outs, boldly and simply drawn. At the end of this period, the theme hymn was first introduced and the children learned the tune and sang the first verse.

The third worship period, at 1.50 p.m., told the story of Mary Magdalen. Verses 1, 2 and 3 of the hymn were sung. At 2.30 p.m. the witnesses used were St John and the Mother of Jesus, and the fourth verse was added to ' our hymn '. For the closing worship period, at 3.15 p.m., parents were invited to attend. The figures of the centurion and of ' us'—a group of adults and children in modern dress—formed the subject of the address. The final mood was one of triumph, anticipating Easter. The last prayer was: ' Dear Lord Jesus, you died bravely because you love us. Help us to live bravely because we love you. Help us to understand your presence with us, so that we can know you as our Friend, our Saviour and our glorious King.' The day concluded with a rousing rendering of ' our hymn ', including the last verse:

> ' What do I see as I look up in prayer?
> What makes my heart want to sing?
> I see a man who is living for ever,
> Jesus the Saviour is King.'

and the children ended this with a joyful shout of ' Hooray! ' that must have nearly raised the roof—as heart-warming a cheer as I have ever heard.

The activities had been so planned that each child would have something to take home to Mum at the end of the day, however simple it might be. The helpers understood how important it was to foster a feeling of achievement; they had skilfully prepared a wide range of crafts and were ready with advice or assistance if it was sought.

Easter gardens could be made from greenery, flowers and pebbles; Easter cards from stencils or with paints and crayons. Older ones could make plaster-of-Paris ornaments, using Plasticine moulds. Ingenious boxes, topped by an Easter chicken, had been pre-cut from stiff card and the folds ready scored. They could be glued together and painted even by the smallest ones. (A pattern for these boxes is given here.) They were then ready to be filled with home made sweets. Moulds, flavourings and food colouring had been provided, as had the simple basic ingredients for fondant icing. Drawn by the music, the children moved quite naturally from noisy activity session to quiet worship. ' Time became our greatest enemy,' said Mr Boar. ' Miss Parry was so right in saying we should be longing for more of it! '

The service had manifestly succeeded in deepening the fellowship in this little group of villages. At the end of the day the children were richer in understanding and in achievement, the helpers exhausted but delighted. Perhaps the whole effort was best summed up by one of them in a memorable remark. ' When we started,' she said, ' we were just a bunch of people who knew each other to say good morning to in church. But when we finished, we were a family.'

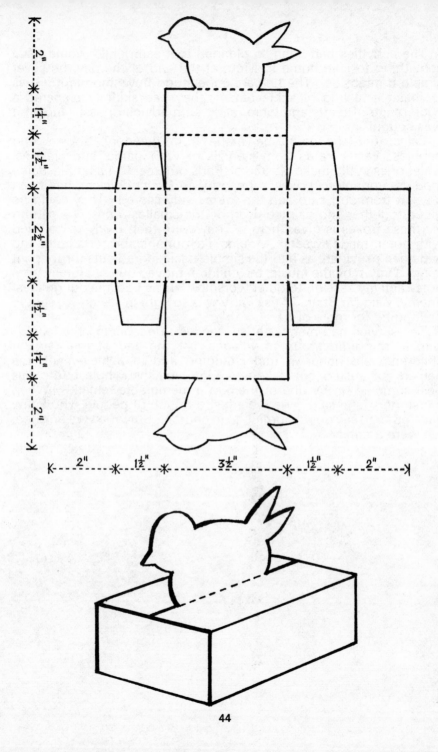

2"

1¼"

1½"

2½"

1½"

1¼"

2"

2" 1½" 3½" 1½" 2"

44

THE FRIDAY CRIME

Music by Jessica Higgs

Words by Elizabeth Hawes

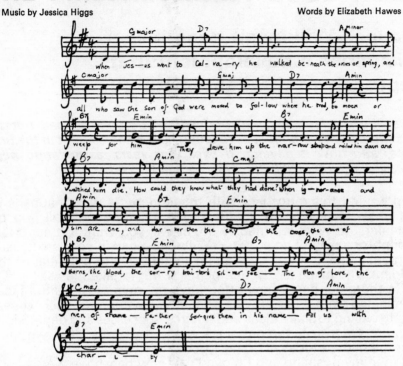

When Jesus went to Calvary
  he walked beneath the skies of spring,
and all who saw the Son of God
were moved to follow where he trod,
to mock, or weep for him.

They drove him up the narrow steep
and nailed him down and watched him die.
How could they know what they had done?—
when ignorance and sin are one,
and darker than the sky.

    The cross, the crown of thorns, the blood,
      the sorry traitor's silver fee,
      the Man of Love, the men of shame—
      Father, forgive them in his name.
      Fill us with charity!

FOUR GOOD FRIDAYS: 1

Frances Wilkinson describes one parish's development in its approach to the Easter liturgy

[The five articles appearing under this title are intended not so much to describe a project as to study how it came about in the first place, and how it developed over four years, assimilating new ideas and younger children. They should be read as a unit.]

I am writing this retrospect with trepidation. Is what happens in one parish ever relevant to the needs of another? Will you be ' listening ' to what we tried to do, or will you want to treat it like a script for a play of your own? Will it fill a gap in your next year's programme, or will you care about the needs and potential of the children who made it? Better, perhaps, not to take the risk!

On the other hand, how often have my own most fruitful ideas germinated from a seed in someone else's written record? Unless we are willing to share ideas and failures, successes and depressions how are we to face the pressures which are on us all as we minister to children today? So here goes!

When my husband and I moved to a new parish we were happy to hear that the full Easter Liturgy was observed. Both his curates were experienced priests, and in Holy Week they undertook his initiation. At the Easter vigil everything was liturgically exquisite. The congregation was minimal. The curates did not feel that it was a service to which one would expect the laity to come in great numbers. Soundings taken afterwards revealed that some had come once and didn't ' like it '; some were ' not as high as that '; a church-warden felt that the word ' vigil ' put people off (knights in cold churches and all that). There was not a grain of imaginative understanding of what the service was about.

The fossil

The following year, parish magazine articles attempted to explain the significance of the Easter liturgy in the life of the church. Personal invitations were given; and the hope was expressed that at least the members of the PCC would be present. Some senior boys

46

were rehearsed in the Canticles and the congregation was encouraged to leave their seats and follow what was happening in the porch; individual candles were issued. The result was a service more satisfying to the vicarage—but we realised that a symbol can become fossilized until no amount of talking about it, or teaching about it can revivify it. In this case, no meaning was any longer attached even to the fossil. Any connection between Easter and Baptism had been entirely lost.

Real re-creation

Meanwhile our Bishop was encouraging people to take this connection seriously. In his Diocesan Letter he wrote: ' It is not simply a matter of getting to what services are planned where you live, but of how to enter as deeply as possible into Christ's sufferings so that you may know fully and joyfully the power of his resurrection.' ... ' the Vigil on Saturday night is perhaps the period which most needs to be guarded, so that " festivities ", so-called, are not allowed to seduce the baptised member of Christ's body from his real re-creation . . . to be restored to the freedom, truth and joy of the baptismal state.' He concluded, ' It is very necessary that clear, simple, direct instruction should be given about how to prepare for this experience, because so many people do not know.'

Our congregation certainly did not know, and did not very much want to know. On Passion Sunday in the third year we still did not know what to do, until suddenly we were seized by the realisation that we were thinking about the wrong people. If symbols were to be revitalised, we must start with the children. We set ourselves one simple goal, to get *families* into church at 8.30 p.m. on Easter Eve.

There was no time to make a complicated plan. Some of the best things one does with children are *ad hoc*. The aim must be clear; the detail devotedly attended to—but in between the Holy Spirit will take a lot of elbow-room if it is left for his use.

On Palm Sunday after Parish Communion everyone under sixteen was asked to stay behind to discuss the possibility of doing something together in Holy Week. Our small junior Sunday school took notes home inviting parents to let children come to church every morning. We did no other canvassing, and the group which materialised was about right for two adult leaders, and remained remarkably constant through the week.

Time together

There are no notes extant about the first discussion which took place that evening with the teen-age children. Memory says that we decided to work towards something which other members of the congregation could share with us on Good Friday; that it would not be a ' performance ', but the result of spending an hour or two together every day thinking ourselves into the events of Holy Week. A scissors-and-paste job was done on the New English Bible (and many other readings and episodes could just as well have been chosen) and we explained the significance of the Easter ceremonies as we went along. We did not use the word ' vigil ' but spoke consistently about ' the lighting of the Easter candle ', we spoke of the many things which had to be done in church this week, and especially on Thursday (when we clean and polish the altars) and on Saturday, the reasons for these and the help which would be needed. We assumed that the older children would not want to ' dress up ', but we encouraged them to see the need of the younger children for movement and costume. Their own best contribution would be in the worthy preparation of the readings and the hymns.

Vows renewed
By the time they went home it was clear that if the Easter candle was to have significance on Easter Eve, there must be a Holy Week candle which was extinguished on Good Friday. It so happened that in a chest in the vestry there was a two-foot-tall stump of an old Paschal candle. By the small hours of the next morning it was clear that this would be throughout the symbol of our Lord; that the theme song would be the hymn, ' It is a thing most wonderful ', and that we would stress that when we sang, ' O light the flame within my heart ', we were singing about something that had already been done in our baptism, and in the context of this, and of the candle, we would, quite concretely, present the significance of our renewal on Saturday night of our baptismal vows.

We were fortunate that we have in our church an apron to the chancel steps, erected by the religious drama people and too troublesome to take down, but otherwise we used our very traditional 19th-century Gothic church just as it was.

Natural movement
During the week the children were encouraged to come quietly into church and say their prayers. Prayers of pith and brevity were attached to the ledges of some pews. During rehearsals perfectly normal voices were used, and no attempt was made to quell exuberance of movement. By Friday there was no trace of the inhibition of ' being in church '. Movement was natural and spontaneous, and real participation and expression was apparent.

On Saturday the boys filled the font to the brim so that the Easter candle would reflect in the water. Girls helped the vicar to dress the altars, and were helped by adults to do flower arrangement. Younger boys collected firewood for the bonfire from which the new fire would be taken.

Throughout the week a greeting was used: ' The Lord has done great things for us ', to which the response was, ' And we are very glad '. When the readers (the teen-age contingent) went to their seats in the choir on Friday morning, they found an envelope containing a post-card sized print of Dali's ' Christ of St John of the Cross ' with an extract from the description of this picture in Douglas Webster's book *In Debt to Christ*. We had referred to this picture throughout the week, impressing upon the children that Jesus was a young man with everything to live for.

The ' Children's Liturgy ' as it emerged for the ' first ' Good Friday will follow.

FOUR GOOD FRIDAYS: 2

The service which emerged for the 'first' Good Friday

Properties
The two-foot stump of an old Paschal candle, which would stand by itself. The two fronds of palm from the Palm Sunday procession. Branches of pussy willow for the younger children.
Simple costume for under 11s.
Water pot. Round flat loaf. Chalice. Small table.
Duplicated hymn sheets for practising, and for the congregation on Good Friday.
White cloth, table, hot cross buns in white napkins.
A small alb for the candle bearer and a white scapular to match.

Two girls playing violas.
The Leaders: two adults.
The Readers: teenagers.

Children's Service
Hymn A. & M. 435 (English Hymnal tune), verses 1 and 3.
> It is a thing most wonderful,
> Almost too wonderful to be,
> That God's own son should come from heaven
> And die to save a child like me.

> I cannot tell how he could love
> A child so weak and full of sin,
> His love must be most wonderful
> If he could die my love to win.

Leader 1: Today is Good Friday, and all over the world Christians are remembering the death of Jesus on the cross. We will think especially today of the girls and boys in [*the Church associated with the Lent Project*] as they too, show their love for the Lord Jesus in their Good Friday service.

Leader 2: Both we, here in St............'s and they, in their church of St............, are preparing for the joy which comes to Christians every year in the celebration of our Lord's victory over death, on Easter Day.

Leader 1: Jesus told us that he is the light of the world. We remind ourselves of this by using candles in church. When Jesus died, there was darkness over the whole land—and so, today in the church there are no candles on the altar, because Jesus is crucified. Tomorrow night the great Easter candle will be lighted, to tell us that he is alive, and with us for ever.

Leader 2: But in our service this morning we shall use a lighted candle, and when the time of his death comes, in the story which we shall tell again, we shall put it out. Those of you who can come with your parents tomorrow night will see the Easter candle lit.

Leader 1: Here then, is the candle, which .... will carry during our service. [*Leader lights the candle, which is carried a few yards down centre aisle.*] When you look at the candle, say to yourself, ' Jesus is my light '. Let us say it now, together.

All: Jesus is my light.

Leader 2: We are going to begin our remembering of Jesus with the story of Palm Sunday.

[*Palm bearers flank candle, forming arch over head of bearer.*]

Reader 1 [*one, two, or more readers to each passage, depending on numbers and blend of voices*]: They were nearing Jerusalem; and Jesus sent two disciples with these instructions: ' Go to the village opposite, where you will find a donkey tethered, which no-one has yet ridden. Untie it, and bring it here. If anyone asks, " Why are you untying it? " say, " Our Master needs it." ' The disciples went and did as Jesus said. They laid their cloaks on the donkey, and Jesus mounted. Crowds of people carpeted the road with their cloaks, and some cut branches from the trees to spread in his path. And the whole company of his friends in their joy began to sing aloud the praise of God.

[*Candle bearer slowly to altar rail, flanked by palms, and followed by all younger children from stations in front pews, waving branches. Candle held high at centre. Children part and face one another, and sing:*]

> The glory of our King was seen
> When he came riding by,
> And all the children waved and sang,
> ' Hosanna, King most high.'

All: Hosanna. Blessed is he who comes in the name of the Lord. Hosanna in the highest.

[*Children return to places, following candle bearer to mid-aisle.*]

Reader 2: Jesus had powerful enemies who hated this welcome, and longed to harm him. Judas, one of his closest friends took money from them, and promised to lead them to him.

Reader 3: But Jesus had important things to do before he was arrested. He did not say where he would be. Instead he used a secret sign. He sent Peter and John, with these instructions: ' Go and prepare for our Passover supper.' ' Where would you like us to make the preparations? ' they asked. ' As soon as you set foot in the city,' he replied, ' a man will meet you, carrying a water jar. Follow him into the house he enters, and the householder will show you a large room upstairs, all set out.' They went, and found everything as he had said. [*Two children in costume follow a third carrying a water pot from back of church. They mount steps, place a small table in the centre, and place on it a loaf and a chalice, and stand on each side.*]

Reader 4: When the time came, he took his place at table.
[*The candle bearer walks down aisle with two more children in costume. Goes behind table and sets the candle down on it, and steps back. Priest stands behind table ready to mime the blessing and breaking of the bread as Reader continues:*]
The apostles sat down with him. And he took bread, and after giving thanks to God, broke it, and said, ' This is my body, which is given for you.' In the same way he took the cup and said, ' Whenever you drink this, do it in remembrance of me. Every time you eat this bread and drink this cup, you proclaim my death.'

All sing: The glory of our King is seen,
In blessed and broken bread.
When Jesus gives himself to us,
And we by him are fed.

Reader 5: And when they had sung a hymn they went out, and he made his way as usual to the Mount of Olives, accompanied by his disciples. [*Candle bearer removes candle from table, which is lifted away by readers. Disciples to side, seated on ground. Candle bearer faces altar, kneeling.*
He withdrew from them about a stone's throw,[1] and knelt down, and prayed that if it were possible he might be spared the test. ' Father,' he said, ' all things are possible to you: spare me this. Yet not as I will, but as you will.' When he rose from

---

[1] We found that the expression ' stone's throw ' conveyed nothing. It is necessary constantly to remember that biblical expressions (and traditional religious ones) need constant paraphrasing. Another example is following Jesus—the trad definition of discipleship. Today you follow the town team, a much more passive operation!

prayer and came back he found his friends sleeping, worn out by grief.

[*Candle bearer rises from knees, turns and returns to disciples.*] And he said, ' Up, let us go forward, my betrayer is upon us.'

[*Candle bearer to edge of platform.*]

Reader: The place was known to Judas, his betrayer, because Jesus often met there with his disciples. He had brought with him a detachment of soldiers and police, provided by the chief priests and the Pharisees, equipped with lanterns, torches and weapons. Judas had given them this sign. ' The one I kiss is your man; seize him.' Jesus went to meet them, and asked, ' Who is it you want? ' Judas stepped forward and said, ' Master,' and kissed him. Jesus said, ' Friend, what are you here to do? ' and to the soldiers he said, ' I am the man you want. Let these others go.' Then they came forward and seized Jesus and held him fast.

[*Candle bearer turns towards altar, with disciples and readers in front of him*].

Reader 7: For twelve long hours Jesus was questioned, bullied, flogged, spat upon and mocked. His friends deserted him. One of the closest of them said he did not know him.

[*Disciples, and children in choir stalls all leave platform, with backs turned to candle, faces averted.*]

At last they put a great cross of wood on his shoulders, and led him out to die.

[*Candle bearer turns, and walks away slowly down North aisle, followed by all the children, heads bowed. (Two children here played the Passion Chorale on violas.) Make a station at the font at west end.*]

Reader 7 [*this reader alone is left on stage*]: On their way they met a man from Africa, and made him carry the cross, because Jesus was exhausted.

[*Procession continues, younger children back into pews. Disciples and older children on to stage, grouped round candle.*]

Reader 7: When they came to a hill called Golgotha, they fastened him to the cross. And as they drove in the nails, Jesus said, ' Father, forgive them: they do not know what they are doing.'

All sing: The glory of our King was seen
When, with his arms stretched wide,
To show his love for everyone,
Jesus was crucified.

Reader 8: For three long hours he hung there, and there was darkness over the whole land.

All sing: On the holy cross I see,
Jesu's arms stretched out for me,
Loving Jesus, let me be
Still and quiet, close to thee,
Learning all thy love for me,
Giving all my love to thee.[1]

[*Younger children mime as they sing.*]

Reader: And at three o'clock, Jesus gave a loud cry, and died.

[*The candle is put out. (The chorale was played again by the violas). The candle bearer carries the candle to one side and places it on the table.*]

All sing: Hymn 435, verses 4, 5, 6, 7:

I sometimes think about the cross
And shut my eyes, and try to see
The cruel nails and crown of thorn
And Jesus, crucified for me.

But even could I see him die
I could but see a little part
Of that great love which like a fire
Is always burning in his heart.

It is most wonderful to know
His love to me so free and sure,
But 'tis more wonderful to see
My love to him so faint and poor.

And yet I want to love thee Lord
O, light the flame within my heart
And I will love thee more and more
Until I see thee as thou art.

Reader 9: And Joseph of Arimathaea bravely went to the Governor, and asked for the body of Jesus; and he bought a linen sheet, and took him down from the cross and wrapped him in the

---

[1] Young children can mime this meaningfully. The original has another couplet which is quite unsuitable for children. We must keep central what the crucifixion meant in love, not in the detail of the suffering, when talking to children.

sheet. Then he laid him in a tomb cut from the rock and rolled a stone across the entrance.

And on the first day of the week the women brought spices to embalm his body.

Leader 1: And now we shall go quietly to the back of the church, and eat together the spiced buns which for hundreds of years Christians have eaten on this day. They have a cross on them, to remind us how Jesus died. They have five currants in them, to remind us of the five wounds he received; and they are spiced to remind us of his burying.

Leader 2 (Priest): And tomorrow we will come back, not with the spices and myrrh which the women brought for his body, but with a glad song of joy and triumph to share with his risen Body, which is the Church in Easter joy. Because the light has shone on in the dark, and the darkness was not able to quench it.

And may the blessing of God almighty, the Father, the Son, and the Holy Spirit, be with you all.

FOUR GOOD FRIDAYS: 3

How the parish's 'Service of New Light' developed in its second and third years of use

(In this article third year additions appear in **heavier type**)

Although the leaders could think of several possible developments, we decided that any radical changes must come from the children themselves to ensure that they were matched by real development of thought. This year the older group, whom we were sure would have jibbed the year before if asked to dress up as for a school Nativity play, were keen to be in costume. This deprived us of readers, so their part was taken by two participating adults. They wanted more action; more use of music; older members of the younger group to act as scene changers; the Palm procession to be accompanied by recorders; the addition of the last supper, in mime.

They were interested in Judas, and wanted to develop his part in the drama. They would introduce a centurion in order the better to mime the arrest, but they were clear that we should stick to the candle as the symbol of Jesus, rather than having an actor for the Christos—' because of the Easter candle '. The adults were a little nervous about this mixture of *genre*—but in the event it was impressive.

They remembered from the year before that the younger children had difficulty in disposing of their palms when they returned to the pews. This year they would place them on the sanctuary step as they passed, and return without them.

The theme-prayer this year was the Prayer of St Richard, which was used at every session, and was printed on the Good Friday card received by all.

At the Service of New Light everyone in church went *outside* and watched the kindling of the fire, and saw the candle marked and lighted in the porch as one of the congregation had seen it done in France. As the candle went through the door, one of the eleven-year-olds greeted it with a trumpet fanfare.

The development in the third year was more in depth than kind. Two senior boys took over the readings. The choir had flourished during the year under an enthusiastic and competent choirmaster, and the children felt they could feed in some of the Good Friday music they had learned. One of the adult participants this year was adept at training, and at movement from here to there; innovations such as the casting of long coloured sashes across the path of the Palm procession were beautifully done. The feet-washing was incorporated, and the action in the mimes showed deepening sensitivity. A roll of thunder was put on to tape.

The emphasis throughout in the third year was on Easter, and a card was given at the Easter Vigil—or, as we were now quite naturally calling it, 'the Service of New Light'. It was B62 of the Community of St. Clare, Freeland, Oxford: 'The Light of Christ, which riseth gloriously, banish all darkness from each heart and mind.' It was doubly appropriate, because some of the young people had had heavy anxiety and sorrow to face during the year, which had been resolved with the support and fellowship of the church.

CHILDREN'S LITURGY FOR GOOD FRIDAY
(Second and third years)

Hymn: A & M 435, verses 1 and 3 (Tune: Herongate, EH 549) ' It is a thing most wonderful.'

Reader 1: Today is Good Friday, and all over the world, Christians are remembering the death of Jesus on the cross.

(The readers in the second year were two adult assistants. In the third year, two teenage boys.)

Reader 2: In secret, in China, where churches are closed, and Christians are in danger.

Reader 1: In churches in India, where congregations are poor and hungry.

(Introductory sentences were built up from news topical at the time.)

Reader 1: In countries where Christians are very few.

Reader 2: And in countries like our own where it is easy to call oneself a Christian and do very little about it.

1 and 2: Together we are preparing for the joy which comes to Christians every year, in the celebration of our Lord's victory over death on Easter day.

[*Solemn music*]

Reader 1: Jesus told us that he is the light of the world. We remind ourselves of this by using candles in Church. When Jesus died, there was darkness over the whole land—and so, today in church, there are no candles on the altar, because Jesus is crucified.
Tomorrow the great Easter candle will be lit, to tell us that he is alive, and with us for ever.

Reader 2: But in our service this morning/**evening** we shall use a lighted candle, and when the time of his death comes, in the story we shall tell again, we shall put it out. Those of you who can come tomorrow night will see the Easter candle lit.

(*In year 1 and 2 this service took the place of the old ' Children's service' on Good Friday morning. The third year it was moved to the evening, for fathers and working members of the congregation. We faced right through that 8.30 p.m. on Saturday night (the earliest possible for a dark church when Easter is late) was not a time we could expect the youngest children to be brought. It was stressed that, once lit, the candle would always be alight at any service their parents could, or would bring them to. One child, bringing mother to see, was disappointed not to find it alight at other times.*)

Reader 1: Here then is the candle, which . . . will carry during our service [*light candle.*] When you look at the candle, say to yourself, ' Jesus is my light '. Let us all say it now, together.

All: Jesus is my light.

[*Candle bearer moves slowly down the centre aisle.*]

Reader 2: We are going to begin our remembering of Jesus with the story of Palm Sunday.

[*Candle at back of church, palm branches flanking, procession of senior children (disciples) in costume, formed behind.*]

Reader 1: They were nearing Jerusalem; and Jesus sent two disciples with these instructions. ' Go to the village opposite, where you will find a donkey tethered, which no one has yet ridden. Untie it and bring it here. If anyone asks you, ' Why are you untying it? ' say, ' Our Master needs it.' The disciples went and did as Jesus said. They laid their cloaks on the donkey, and Jesus mounted.

[*For small boys of the cowboy age and for older children of sensitive understanding it helps to be reminded of the normal behaviour of unbroken colts; and the remark of the cowboy*] *in the wild west who, on hearing the story said, ' What hands the man must have had! ']*

[Procession begins to come down aisle. Younger children with branches of pussy willow leave choir stalls, and come out on apron stage to meet it.]

[Two children fling lengths of brilliant cloth in the path of the procession.]

Crowds of people carpeted the road with their cloaks, and some cut branches from the trees to spread in his path. And the whole company of his friends in their joy began to sing aloud the praise of God.

[Candle bearer to altar rail, flanked by palms, followed by procession. Candle held high at centre. Part and face one another, and sing:]

> The glory of our King was seen,
> When he came riding by,
> And all the people waved and sang,
> Hosanna, King most high.

> (EH 428. Tune: Dundee)

All *[waving branches]*: Blessed is he who comes in the name of the Lord. Hosanna in the highest.

[Candle bearer turns, and moves west. Others follow, depositing branches on the sanctuary steps as they pass. Procession moves slowly and solemnly in contrast to first sweeping movement. Judas leaves the procession to right of apron. Small children into front pews. Leave two children in choir stalls to prepare upper room.]

Reader 2: Jesus had powerful enemies who hated this welcome, and longed to harm him. Judas, one of his closest friends, wishing to force Jesus to show his power, promised to lead them to him.

(This they decided in discussion, was the most likely reason for Judas' defection. They were doubtful about the money motive—it is difficult to make thirty pieces of silver seem more than £15—and, given a man who would betray his friend like this, they did not think he would feel sufficient remorse for suicide unless something had gone very seriously wrong with his plans.)

Reader 2: But Jesus had important things to do before he was arrested. He did not say where he would be. He said to Peter and John, ' Go and prepare our Passover supper '. ' Where would you like us to make the preparations,' they asked. ' As soon as you set foot in the city,' he replied, ' a man will meet you, carrying a water jar. Follow him into the house he enters, and the householder will show you a large upper room all set out '. They went and found everything as he had said.

(The ' secret signs ' of Holy Week are useful teaching points. Juniors love them, and seniors find through them a realisation of the extent to which Jesus remained in control of the situation until everything was ready for its consummation.)

[During this reading, the two children left in the choir stalls quickly prepare the upper room. (We were fortunate to have 13 tiny nursery chairs, which just spanned the space available.) Table [**ewer, basin and towel**]*.*

[At ' As soon as . . .' Peter and John set out, east, preceded by the water carrier, to the platform. Water carrier goes off, left. Peter and John place chalice and loaf on table, and stand, centre.]

Reader 2: When the time came *[disciples follow candle down aisle]* he took his place at table. And the disciples sat down with him. *[The candle is stood on the table, and the bearer mimes the action. Judas must sit at the end of the semi-circle of disciples, for an easy get-away.]*

Reader 1: And during supper, Jesus rose from the table, and taking a towel tied it round him. Then he poured water into the basin, and began to wash his disciples' feet and wipe them with the towel.

[**Mime throughout**]

Reader 2: *[Mime throughout]* And he took the cup, and after giving thanks, he said: ' Take this, and share it among yourselves ' *[cup passed from hand to hand]*. And he took bread, gave thanks and broke it, and gave it to them with the words, ' This is my body '.

[Judas receives the bread first, gets up and departs.]

Reader 2: And when Judas had received the bread he went out . . . and it was night.

[The third year, the teenager reading these four words made a deep impression of desolation.]

Sing: The glory of our King is seen
In blessed and broken bread,
When Jesus gives himself to us,
And we by him are fed.
[*This verse does not appear in the original hymn. It was invented to give a tidy appearance to the treatment of the important events. While this verse is sung the disciples get up and move their chairs to one side.*]

Reader 1: And when they had sung a hymn they went out, and he made his way as usual to the Mount of Olives, accompanied by his disciples.
[*Candle moves half-way down chancel. Disciples to communion rail, where they sit in a group, with heads on knees.*]

Reader 1: And he withdrew from them a short distance, and knelt down [*candle bearer kneels*] and prayed that if it were possible, he might be spared the test. ' Father,' he said, ' all things are possible to you; spare me this. Yet not as I will, but as you will.' His disciples slept, worn out by grief.

Reader 2: The place was known to Judas, his betrayer, because Jesus often met there with his disciples.
[*Judas and centurion come down aisle.*]
He brought with him a detachment of soldiers and police, equipped with lanterns, torches and weapons. (*These could, of course, be introduced if there were sufficient children and costume. But care needs to be taken of the children who take ' bad' parts. The aim is not to produce a realistic drama but to give opportunities for identification.*)
[*Disciples rise quickly and disperse into choir stalls.*]
Jesus went to meet them, and said, ' Who is it you want? '
[*Candle to mid-apron.*]
and he said to Judas, ' Friend, what are you here to do? ' and to the soldiers he said, ' I am the man you want. Let the others go.' And they came forward and held him fast.
[*Centurion places hand on candle-bearer's shoulder.*]

Reader 1: And all the disciples forsook him and fled.
[*Disciples off stage with averted faces; viola players to side where instruments are ready.*
Candle bearer turns to altar. Centurion stands by.
The disciples take station at floor level and remain in a group as the crowd.]

Sing: O Holy Jesus, how hast thou offended?
(*The third year we had help from a musician.*)

Reader 2: For twelve long hours, Jesus was questioned, bullied, flogged, spat upon and mocked.

Congregational hymn: O dearest Lord, thy sacred head (A & M 436).

Reader 1: At last they put a heavy cross on his shoulders, and led him out to die.
[*Candle bearer and centurion followed by two Marys and John walk away slowly down north aisle, followed by all the company, heads bowed. Make a station at the font.*]
[*In the third year some small children in the congregation spontaneously left their seats and joined the procession, rejoining their parents afterwards.*]

Reader 2: On their way they met a man from Africa and the soldiers made him carry the cross, because Jesus was exhausted.
[*Procession down central aisle. Younger children into pews. Older ones in group at foot of step. Two Marys and John on platform to sides and front of candle bearer (who faces altar) and centurion.*]

Reader 1: And when they came to Golgotha/**Skull Hill** [*Third year alteration. It tells us what Golgotha means, so why don't we use it? It sounds like a real name*], they fastened him to the cross, and as they drove in the nails, Jesus said, ' Father, forgive them. They do not know what they are doing.'

Sing: The glory of our King was seen
When, with his arms spread wide,
To show his love to everyone,
Jesus was crucified.

Reader 2: For six long hours he hung there, and there was darkness over the whole land.
[Thunder roll on tape.]

Sing: **On the holy cross I see**
Jesu's arms stretched out for me.
Loving Jesus, let me be
Still and quiet, close to thee.
Learning all thy love for me.
Giving all my love to thee.
[*See footnote to second article*]

Reader 2: And at three o'clock, Jesus gave a loud cry, and died. [*The centurion extinguishes the candle. The candle bearer places it on the small table to side and retires into choir stalls.*]

Hymn: A & M 434, verses 4, 5, 6, 7. ' I sometimes think about the cross.'

Reader 2: And Joseph of Arimathaea bravely went to the Governor, and asked for the body of Jesus; and he bought a linen sheet, and took the body down from the cross, and wrapped it in the sheet.

[*Joseph comes on to stage, takes candle and carries it to bare altar.*]

And on the first day of the week, the women brought spices to embalm his body.

[*The women come on to the platform and stand in tableau.*]

Reader 1: And now we shall go quietly to the back of the church, and eat together the spiced buns which, for hundreds of years Christians have eaten on Good Friday. They have a cross on them, to remind us how Jesus died. They have five currants in them, to remind us of the five wounds he received, and they are spiced to remind us of his burying.

(*Since the second year these have been made by one of the parents. If more than one parent is involved specify the recipe. There should be sufficient for all the participants, and for all children, however small, who come as part of the congregation. Ours were brought down hot from the Vicarage oven by people who slipped out at an appropriate point. They were served in white napkins.*)

Reader 2: And tomorrow we shall come back, not with the spices and myrrh which the women brought for his body, but with a glad song of joy and triumph, to share, with his risen body the Church, in Easter joy because the light has shone on in the dark, and the darkness has not been able to quench it.

Reader 1: And now may the love of the Lord Jesus draw us to himself.
May the power of the Lord Jesus strengthen us to serve him.
And may the joy of the Lord Jesus fill our hearts.

All: Thanks be to God.

FOUR GOOD FRIDAYS: 4

How a weekend course for young people evolved out of the now familiar Holy Week service

We had a difficult problem in the fourth year. Some of the original members of the older group were now over seventeen, and for them this very simple treatment needed developing. We were woefully short of leadership, all but one of the former adult participants having moved away from a parish involved in social upheaval. It was difficult to see how we could separate the activity for under 11s and over 11s, let alone seniors, and still do something worth while.

We solved our problem with the help of a Religious Drama Group producer who had produced *Mann's End* with the same group a few years earlier: for 15s to 18s, work through Lent on a production of *Casey* by P. W. Turner, to be performed on Good Friday, followed by a residential weekend at a conference house over Low Sunday. We felt this would give ample opportunity for consolidating what had gone before, in understanding and worship. As Lent went on there was no doubt that *Casey* was digesting and bringing up to date the work of the last three years. The production, on the evening of Good Friday was extremely impressive; and the challenge of John, the West Indian, singularly appropriate, as by this time a high percentage of immigrants were resident in our own parish.

Symbol of the book

We had to face the fact that a Holy Week course for under 13s would be impracticable this year, and decided that their climax must come on Palm Sunday. We could presume that the Good Friday Service (as we had done it before) was well in the mind of the older members of this group, and that co-operation which did not require much rehearsal would be readily forthcoming from the 13s to 18s. The details of the Palm Sunday story were found to be fairly well known, and with a miscellaneous collection of former participants, Cubs, Brownies, and junior choir, we set about working out a simple but impressive children's liturgy for Palm Sunday.

The use of a symbol to represent our Lord having been so well understood and so impressive in our other experiments, we decided to use, as the symbol of his presence in the procession, the red Gospel book, carried by the celebrant. This was explained to the Parish Communion congregation at the beginning of the service. Wherever the Book was carried they were to imagine our Lord on the first Palm Sunday. Before the service the younger children did not go to the pews, but waited quietly in the narthex at the back of the church with their branches of pussy willow. The older children who were *not* in the choir went to sit in the choir stalls.

Procession of palms

After the blessing and distribution of the Palms, the Procession set off as usual down the south aisle: Crucifer, palm bearers, junior choir (without hymn-books), senior choir, light-bearers, celebrant.

At the west end of the aisle the senior choir halted, and the juniors went on round to the font at the west end, where they collected their ' palm '. The rest of the waiting children joined in behind them, in front of the seniors, and they all continued in procession, singing ' All glory, laud, and honour ', down the central aisle, up the north aisle, to the font again.

Here the crucifer moved aside; the senior procession left the rest and walked in silence down the centre aisle, and into the choir stalls, where the lights were put out.

The lights and the celebrant then moved in front of the younger children, who immediately burst into shouts of ' Hosanna, Blessed is he who comes in the name of the Lord '. They followed the Book to the chancel steps. Here there was a silent pause, broken by shouts of ' Crucify! Crucify! ' from the seniors in the darkened chancel, waving clenched fists. The crucifer and the Book moved firmly on into the chancel, while the children lowered their palms, slinking away into the safety of the pews in various parts of the church.

An elderly member of the congregation said afterwards that she had never realised before ' how it must have been '.

The prayer throughout the rehearsals for *Casey* was:

> ' Wherever thy glory may be best served,
> Whenever, however,
> There, then, and in that place,
> May I thy servant be.'

and the card was a National Gallery postcard of van Honthorst's ' Christ before the High Priest '.

Perhaps the best way of indicating how all of this was tied up at the residential week-end is to borrow, from the parish magazine, the report which one of the leaders put together afterwards for the benefit of the older members of the congregation. The material of the final service which is mentioned below will next month form the fifth and last of this series of articles.

Points of view

' On arrival members of the group were asked to write down a question which they would like to ask the Vicar/the organist/the secretary of the Mothers' Union/the Parish Centre Management Committee, etc. The questions were interesting and responsible, in some cases illuminating; and after supper we divided into groups and tried to answer the questions, with leaders contributing on matters of fact. This was good experience in trying to understand other people's points of view, and a lot of sensible suggestions were thrown in. Later, groups re-assembled and discussed what they would miss about their church if they went away; what they would look for in another church; and what action they would take if they found themselves in a church with no equivalent group of young churchmen. One interesting thing which transpired was that they regarded the Easter Service of New Light as a " new approach " to religion, of which they approved. It is, in fact, one of the oldest things which happen in church, but we have tried, largely with their help, to recapture in the last few years, the domesticity and spontaneity with which it would have been celebrated in the early church.

' Saturday morning was devoted to " Workshops " in age-groups; and after an early lunch we went into the nearby town for field-work. Groups of four visited five parish churches to do detective work, and in the evening extremely interesting reports were given on their findings. Some had been to churches where money was no object; some had found themselves confronted by impressive budgets for overseas work; some had interviewed Vicars, and we gathered one had been given advice on starting a Betweens' Group! All groups had noted things one does not always bother to notice about one's own parish church—standards of cleaning; state of hymn books; indications of lay participation; adequacy of notice boards. One group, visiting a church of great magnificence, returned the report that if there are six candles on the altar, all of great size, the Easter candle seems dwarfed and insignificant, and that in fact liturgical worship must always leave a bit in hand to be called on in major Festivals (for our own sakes, not God's).

Ready to take part

' On Sunday morning, after an early celebration of the Eucharist in the chapel, leaders and members spent half an hour quietly circulating round a display of large pictures illustrating the way of the Cross in terms of humanity in the modern world, and writing anonymously about any picture which said anything to them. While other work went on, these contributions, many of them of a high quality of sensitivity and expression, were collated into a sequence, and for our closing act of worship members of the conference read, unrehearsed, the relevant contributions, while the pictures were displayed on the altar. If there is one thing which strikes one about modern educational approaches it is how well almost all children read aloud these days, as compared with those of ten years ago; and the matter-of-fact way in which they participate without self-consciousness or persuasion. No-one present could have left the chapel unmoved; though what God said to each one of us will have been different.'

' We really delved deeply into Christianity—got right into it ' said one of the Reaction Sheets at the end of the week-end. One has often thought of this, as one has watched them reacting to the pressures of the Sixth form, to anxieties about ' places ', and now to college and university. At least we gave them this—and the rest is with God.

FOUR GOOD FRIDAYS: 5

Frances Wilkinson introduces some deeply moving meditations by the group of young people

The pictures used at our week-end conference were a series of 15 superb Photo Visuals from Geo. A. Pflaum, Publisher, Inc., 38 West Fifth Street, Dayton, Ohio, 45402, USA, entitled *The Way of the Cross*. These are obtainable from St Paul's Book Centre, 57 Kensington Church Street, London W8, telephone 01–937 4014.

In this series, each station of the Cross has a picture interpreting the Passion of Christ in modern terms. It would not, I think, be impossible over a period to collect suitable pictures for one's own sequence from material produced in this country using newspapers, magazines, and missionary societies' material.

We mounted the pictures with their captions (separately) on hardboard for preservation and manoeuvrability, but the resulting stack was heavy, and less durable mounting might be more practical.

The pictures were displayed on sills and tables in the conference rooms, and we all, leaders and teenagers from 13 to 18, spent half an hour wandering among them and anonymously jotting down our meditations. There was no sign that this lengthy silence was a strain on anyone. Movement was free, and they were told that it was their own choice whether they wrote anything at all, or how many pictures they chose to consider.

When coffee came, the conference engaged in lighter activities while one leader took the scripts off and, without tampering with the wording or meaning of what had been written, strung together things that had been written about each picture. At the closing service, the script for each picture was issued to a member of the conference, and they were read in sequence as the leader displayed each picture before the altar.

Four pictures had attracted no comment at all—either being outside the young people's experience, or too undramatic for their age. The most moving meditation came from an 18-year-old on the second Station. He walks now with only a slight limp, but has behind him years of acute suffering from osteomyelitis, and years in hospital. The picture attracting the most comment was the twelfth.

As it is not possible to reproduce the pictures, a brief description of each must suffice.

Introduction

The Way of the Cross is only one episode in the unending human journey through suffering. From the hopeless despair there is hope:

> The care of a mother
> The support of a family
> The consolation of a friend.

With each sin we make anew the way of the Cross for ourselves and others until the world seems set on a descending spiral of gloom and despondency. How we lack the Easter joy and victory! We are accustomed to despair and accept it so easily. We must extend the moments of joy, but how?

The first station: Jesus is condemned to die

A poor white family in the southern States. Seven ragged children and a wan mother outside a derelict shack.

The way of the Cross is thrust upon some people.

> The army advances
> The bombs come
> You can't get out
> You live in squalor
> There is no hope of a decent house.

For you the Cross means refusing to be bitter. Fighting the thing itself and praying for those who cause it.

Others seem able to avoid it.

> They are offered protection
> liberation
> freedom
> They can take it, so could Jesus have done.

For them the way means refusing the way out, and looking for the way through. Believing that at the end of a tunnel there is light.

The second Station: Jesus takes up his cross

A mother and father on a hospital verandah watch a smiling nine-year-old managing his crutches after the amputation of his left leg.

For those who do not know, the picture speaks of joy and courage—a happy little chap, proudly showing his prowess to those who are proud of him.

It does not speak of the real Cross.
of the long days and nights of pain,
of the anxieties and tensions of his family,
of the struggle against self-pity,
of the fear of rejection,
of the whole new world of life which must be conquered
when one is crippled
of the desperate fear of helplessness
and the despair in being treated as a young child.

It is these things you must think of when you see this picture of victory.
Here is life—and the support of friends and relatives, and strangers.
The bond of death is being broken here, in life.
Thanks be to God who gives us victory through Christ who won.

The third station: Jesus falls the first time

A Vietnamese family, mother, two children and a baby, with horror on their faces as they realise that the fallen father is dead.

The shattering, numbing, agonising shock.
The sickening fears of months now a reality.
Why me? Why my husband? out of all those people—
One moment a virile young man—
Seconds later—a body, his face twisted with pain, hand
gesturing in the final moments of despair and suffering.
And children crying, out of fear,
too young to understand,
and yet their faces reflecting a lifetime's suffering.
' Little children, love one another, for God is love.'
The shock, the grief, will in due time diminish
But will life ever be the same again?

The fourth Station: Jesus meets his mother

A mother's arm encircling a sorrowful child's head. Not a very clear picture. No comment.

The fifth Station: Simon helps Jesus to carry his cross
The back view of two young boys arms round one another's shoulders, going to school.

This is a picture about friends
Jesus had been a friend to everybody
He was not choosy
He had no prejudice
Perhaps he would have succeeded better had he been more selective.

But this episode is about strangers too. After all his life of compassion, there was only Simon to help him. And Simon was lonely too. Did anyone jump out of the crowd to help him with his heavy load? No—he was black; made for burdens. The soldiers knew it—the crowd knew it, who cared?
The friends of Christ can be lonely people.

The sixth Station: Veronica wipes the face of Jesus
A mother with a baby on her knee and a flannel in her hand. Older child standing by to help. No comment.

The seventh Station: Jesus falls the second time
Child at a school table, doing a test. No comment.

The eighth Station: Jesus meets the women and children
The picture is a photograph of black robed women weeping in the streets. Probably Greek—so remote from their experience as not to be modern. No comment.

The ninth Station: Jesus falls the third time
Vietnamese child in air-raid.

She has lived ever since she was born in a country of continuous war. Whatever the future for her, this fear will be there at the back of her mind. We know she needs love, and security. She is afraid of the whole world.

This is what makes this picture stand out.
So many people are afraid.
She symbolises the suffering of Christ
    She is so beautiful
    but her face is screwed up in pain
It makes an impact on us when we look at it
What kind of impact does the Cross make on me?

The tenth Station: Jesus is stripped of his garments
Close up of an old, worn, battered boots.

Jesus was like these boots. At first he was favoured—then he was disliked, and at the end discarded. Boots can't feel; they do not experience rejection. But Jesus felt the poisoning of people's minds against him.

Old boots
Muddy, bulging,
They have been a long way,
And worn by many feet,
I shouldn't wonder.

Polished and purposeful
Clogging down the street early,
To a good job
Bringing home the wages
To a family
Comfortable, having good holidays.

Sent, down at heel,
To a jumble sale,
Worn to the labour exchange
Hopeless and depressed
Discarded when the tide turned
Thrown out when we wanted to forget.

Picked up by a tramp
Lost—with no hope
No ambition any more—
Accepting
Things as they come
But with no more
belief in life.

And in them all the time
The feet
of Christ the Son of Man
In joy
In sorrow
and in despair
Walking the way of Calvary
How *beautiful* are his feet.

The eleventh Station: Jesus is nailed to the cross
A child being given a hypodermic injection.

Such a little pain—
    though he is obviously feeling it
Perhaps in course of time he will get used to it—
It will become an everyday thing
Like cleaning your teeth
We get used to the idea of Jesus nailed to the cross
But the child is afraid, too—and lonely. He will not know the
doctors and nurses. They are hurting him. He does not understand
their help and their compassion.
O Lord, help us to stand on both sides of the gate of suffering.
With courage and compassion.

The twelfth Station: Jesus dies on the cross
*A stationary car, with a bicycle lying buckled beside it. Police and
spectators in the background. A priest kneels beside the covered
corpse of a young boy. He is making the sign of the cross on his
forehead.*

Death is the immovable object in the path of life. Are we to say
we have defeated death because a man rose from the dead?
Are we to live, and learn, and then be wasted—in a second of
time finished?
Or is death entry into a new life? a spiritual life? Is there a goal
in dying?
Is death the Utopia, the Shangri-La, the end of•pain and
anguish? The end, the farewell?
Or is it the entrance to an everlasting dawn out of an everlasting
sunset?
Why do we feel the shrouded body, with the priest kneeling by
it, is so significant, if this is the end?
The priest, the onlookers are powerless against death; they are
at its mercy. The driver, even if guiltless, will never be the same again.
And in this helplessness the priest makes the sign of the Cross

because
In this sign we conquer
                    —even death.
                The priest speaks
Receive this life into thy hands of care
It is an offering enforced by circumstances beyond control.
In this confusion of hope and destruction
We minister in thy Name,
And I shall have to go and see his mother.

73

Death is inescapable
When?
No-one knows
Tomorrow, next week, next year?
Even today.

Jesus showed us how to bear ourselves towards death. But are we equal to him?

Can we die as he died?
Yes

Are we prepared to give our lives for him?
Yes

For Jesus lives.

The thirteenth Station: Jesus is taken down from the cross
A fireman with a child in his arms

Suffering, pain and death are in his face, and blood streams down it—he has been through water and fire to save the child. It will happen again today, tomorrow, for ever; the pain with which salvation is accomplished.

' Does Christ not suffer whenever one of his children suffer? '
Can we escape being involved in the pain of his suffering?

The fourteenth Station: Jesus is laid in the tomb
The window of an abandoned house, nailed over with planks of wood.

Finished, done with, boarded up, ready for demolition.
When you're croaked, you're croaked. (*A quotation from
    ' Casey '*)
No future here.
No past either
From the look of it.
This kind of shack
never believed in itself
or in its life;
gave nothing
stood for nothing
It waits
for dereliction
and demolition.

It is finished

The last picture

The final picture in the series is of a small girl full of life, running towards us through a cornfield, her arms stretched out, the sun on her face.

But here is life
Out of death and suffering
The child, won in the pain of childbirth,
The wheat, living abundantly in each stalk
Because the grain died.
In Christ
Shall be made alive
Out of the fear of ugliness of death
Comes springing life
                      It is accomplished
But here is something else
A harvest to be reaped
A child
To be brought up, and taught, and kept in joy.
                      Thanks be to God.

'OUT OF THE DEPTHS . . .'

Three poems by young voluntary teachers in Blackburn diocese, exploring the theme of happiness and sadness, in preparation for Good Friday and Easter

Reflections
(written after the news of the death of three teenage soldiers in Belfast.)

Alone in a desolate and bleak world,
I find myself faced with a contrast.
The memories re-echo around my mind
Before it was happiness, happiness.
I was living in a world surrounded with joy,
Never thinking it would happen to me.
But now it has
Too late.
And all that are left are memories, memories.
In this world we stand up for our rights
But is it worth the lives of our loved ones?
Yesterday happiness,
Today emptiness.
This is the price of war.

Empty Houses

Black is the line against the sky
Factories whose chimneys pour
Black, filthy smoke over the
Never ending rows of terraced houses.
The smoke blackened buildings
Stand out like scabby sores
Against the tall, clean blocks of flats
In the modern redevelopments.
Men with their bulldozers and machines
Crash and tear through the empty buildings.

One man's new plan destroying
The dreams of others.
The sharp projection of stones where
Half a row has been torn down
The old torn wallpaper hangs, or flaps
Wildly in the wind.
And the old fireplace on the first floor
Seems to be hung half way up the wall.

On days when no work is done
And there is no noise except
For the wind and an occasional passing car
The streets are deserted.
And the world is empty.
These are the shells where people once lived
But the time has made them leave
For the tall buildings of light.
And the life has now been taken
From the terraced rows.
As the people left,
Life left,
And the shells are dead and useless.

The sadness of slums

A child peers out of the filthy pane
And looks outside at the streaming rain.
The world passes by,
The child starts to cry.
Does nobody care if we live or die?

Her face reflects her inward pain
She looks for her mother down the lane,
But no-one comes,
Is it because we live in the slums
Does nobody care if we live or die?

A woman hobbles down the street.
The child rushes out to greet
    her bedraggled mother,
But where is her father?
Does nobody care if we live or die?

To offset this sadness and recall a mood of joy, a poem from a different source, written by a six year old girl:

spring spring a beautiful time
blossom floats about
and red and yellow flowers
all spring out
spring spring a beautiful time
grass is fresh and new
everyone is happy
and I am too

SOME VERY STRANGE HAPPENINGS IN JERUSALEM

were the subject of this 'televised documentary' presented in church by the children of St Matthew's, Braithwaite, Yorks—(SMB TV)

Cast: Chairman; 1st and 2nd Commentators [*all in modern dress*]; Mr Jacob, a landowner; Mr Isaac, a Temple stall-holder; Mr X, a follower of Jesus; Mary Magdalene [*all in simple Palestinian costume*]

Slides: Homemade titles and views of places mentioned at points in the text. These could be borrowed from tourists or bought from the Bible Lands Society, The Old Kiln, Hazlemere, High Wycombe, Bucks.

Prelude [immediately following short service]
The following tape-recorded material was played:

1. Signal: ' Will all *World in Focus* personnel please go to Studio Four immediately.' [*Repeated. Boys and Girls get up from congregation and start to assemble the studio—see sketch of layout.*]

2. Voice: ' Two minutes to transmission.'

3. Another voice: ' Checking Camera One. Camera One OK? ' [*Cameraman gives thumbs-up sign. Voice and action repeated for Camera Two.*]

4. Voice: ' 25 seconds to transmission.'

5. Station call sign: ' This is SMB TV in colour. Stay tuned for *World in Focus* '.

6. Genuine TV commercial (taped from ITV). Voice: ' Stand by, Studio Four '.

7. Another voice: ' Ten seconds, nine, eight, seven . . .' [*Title caption, slide no. 1, appears on projector*] ' six, five, four, three, two, Sound . . . Programme.'

8. Signature tune.

LAYOUT OF STUDIO 4.

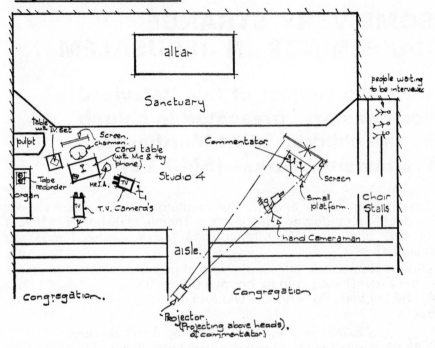

Chairman: Good evening, ladies and gentlemen, welcome to another edition of *World in Focus*.

This week we are going to Palestine, to Jerusalem to be precise, to report on some very strange happenings involving a Nazarene carpenter called Jesus bar Joseph, a man loved by many ordinary people, but hated by the Temple authorities.

The authorities say he claimed to be the Son of God, a blasphemy, a capital offence by Jewish Law. They put him on trial, condemned him, and put him to death. But that's not all. To hear more about the life and death, and some say the resurrection, of this Jesus, over to our commentator outside the main gates of Jerusalem. Come in, commentator A...

[*Slide No. 2 on projector.*]

1st Commentator: Hello, this is A... reporting from the main gates of Jerusalem.

There were exciting scenes here on the outskirts of this great city, on the Sunday before the Passover Feast. This is the feast that the Jewish people keep to celebrate their independence from Egyptian domination.

As usual at this time many pilgrims were on the road, all excited about the forthcoming festivities; the road was crammed with people, carts, horses and donkeys. Then this man Jesus of Nazareth came riding a white donkey up the road with many of his followers. The crowd around him seemed to go mad with excitement.

I am sure many thought him to be the Messiah, the Soldier King whom the Jews believe will one day come to free them from the Romans.

This is the same Jesus who has been causing quite a stir up and down the country.ᐧ He has clashed with the temple and synagogue authorities on a number of occasions.

Some people say that he has performed many miracles, curing many of the sick, making the blind see, and the lame walk, and some that he fed thousands of the poor with no more than a few loaves and one or two fishes. Some believe he has even brought the dead back to life, but you know how people exaggerate, especially simple country folk.

I have with me Mr Jacob, who owns land by the side of the main Jerusalem road.

Tell me, Mr Jacob, what was it like that day?

Mr Jacob: Well, it was very noisy for a start. Mind you, it always is when the pilgrims are coming to the city, singing psalms and hymns of praise to God, and all that.

But when this Jesus chap came up the road they seemed to go daft, some started to put their coats in the road for the donkey to walk on, and just about everyone was shouting, ' Hosanna, God bless him who comes in the name of the Lord, God bless the King of Israel! '

Then a lot of them started to tear down branches from my trees and waved them in the air as they went along. Blooming vandals, made a right mess of MY trees!

Only chap who was quiet was Jesus himself. He sat on that donkey looking a bit sad and lonely, as though he wished it all wasn't happening.

1st Commentator: Well, thank you, Mr Jacob [*turning to camera*]. Many people thought that there would be trouble in the city that night, but nothing happened. Some reports say that Jesus bar Joseph left the city quietly and spent the night with friends at Bethany, a little village not far away. Now back to [*names Chairman*] in the studio.

Chairman: As we now know, it was the following day that there was trouble in Jerusalem, in the temple of all places. Commentator B . . . is outside the temple, ready to tell us about it. Over to commentator B . . . .

[*Slide No. 3 on projector*]

2nd Commentator: Yes! Just inside here on Monday there was trouble. Jesus entered the courtyard which is supposed to be for Gentiles, non-Jews, to come and worship, but in actual fact is a market for selling animals and birds for sacrifice, and this is quite a racket. If you're in on it, you can get very high prices, because only animals from here are accepted by the priests.

Just what did happen, Mr Isaac, a stall-holder who sells pigeons, is going to tell.

Mr Isaac: This trouble-maker Jesus came in shouting something about us making the temple into a den of thieves. He started turning the stalls over and chasing us out with a whip! All my pigeons got away. Cost me a packet. Who does this chap think he is? It's getting so a chap can't earn an honest penny. Time the authorities did something!

2nd Commentator [*quickly*]: Thank you, Mr Isaac. The temple police did not arrest the carpenter at this time; I suppose in all the upset, Jesus slipped away. Now back to the studio.

Chairman: Now the authorities were after him. You can do most things and get away with it, but start hurting people's pockets, and they will get you.

Jesus was seen in the city during the rest of the week, at times back in the temple, in argument with the Pharisees, and there were reports that one of Jesus's followers was in league with them.

I have here in the studio a secret follower of the carpenter, but as he is well-to-do in the city, he wishes to remain anonymous, and will sit with his back to the camera. He is going to tell us what happened just before Jesus was arrested, on Thursday night and Friday morning.

Mr X: On the Thursday evening Jesus arranged that he and his closest friends should eat the passover meal early in their secret meeting-place; this was on the first floor of a building in the city centre.

I was not present myself, but have been told of what happened.

Jesus at this point seemingly knew that one of those there was to let him down and help the authorities in his arrest.

During the course of the evening some of the disciples were arguing as to who would have the best positions in the new kingdom. Jesus took a bowl and a towel and started to wash their feet. Some objected, saying it was beneath Jesus's dignity to wash their feet, but he answered by saying that the greatest in the kingdom of God were the ones who served others.

While they were eating the meal, Jesus took the bread, blessed it, broke it, and gave it to his disciples. ' Take it,' he said, ' this is my body.' Then he took the cup, gave thanks to God and gave it to them; and they all drank from it. Jesus said: ' This is my blood which is poured out for many; my blood seals God's new covenant with you.'

Chairman: What did he mean by all that?

Mr X: At the time I don't think any one knew, but now, looking back on all that's happened, I think he meant this:

That in being crucified he was the sacrifice for us all. He was like a lamb sacrificed in the temple, but for us all. As we Jewish people believed that sacrificing an animal to God can take away sin, so with the greater sacrifice of Jesus it is no longer necessary to sacrifice lambs and pigeons to show God we are sorry for some wrongdoing. What is necessary is belief in Jesus, and true repentance.

Chairman: This is all beyond me! What happened next?

Mr X: He talked a little more—said he was giving them another commandment.

Chairman: What was that?

Mr X: He said we were to love one another.

Chairman: Easier said than done! What next?

Mr X: They sang the Passover hymn, and then they went out for a walk in a near-by orchard. Jesus spent a long time in prayer alone. Then soldiers came to arrest him, led to the spot by Judas.

Chairman: This Judas was a follower of the carpenter?

Mr X: Yes he was, he had slipped away from the supper party earlier.

Chairman: Thank you, Mr X, for coming along to the studio with your story.

Commentator A . . . was at the trial, and we go over to him outside Pilate's Headquarters.

[*Slide No. 4*]

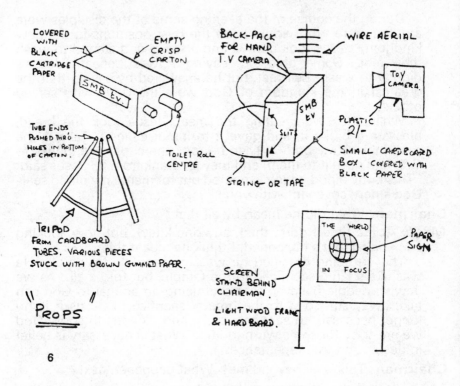

COVERED WITH BLACK CARTRIDGE PAPER

EMPTY CRISP CARTON

BACK-PACK FOR HAND T.V CAMERA

WIRE AERIAL

SMB tv.

TOY CAMERA

SMB tv

SLITS

PLASTIC 2/-

TUBE ENDS PUSHED THRO' HOLES IN BOTTOM OF CARTON.

TOILET ROLL CENTRE

SMALL CARDBOARD BOX. COVERED WITH BLACK PAPER

STRING OR TAPE

TRIPOD FROM CARDBOARD TUBES. VARIOUS PIECES STUCK WITH BROWN GUMMED PAPER.

THE WORLD

PAPER SIGN

IN FOCUS

SCREEN STAND BEHIND CHAIRMAN.

LIGHT WOOD FRAME & HARD BOARD.

" PROPS "

6

1st Commentator: When day came, the elders of the Jews, the chief priests and teachers of the law, met together and Jesus was brought before them. 'Tell us,' they said, 'are you the Messiah?' The carpenter said, 'If I tell you, you will not believe me, but from now on the Son of Man will be seated at the right hand of Almighty God.' They all said, 'Are you, then, the Son of God?' He answered, 'You say I am.' 'We don't need witnesses, we've heard it ourselves,' they said. So then they brought him to the Roman governor, Pilate.

Pilate didn't want to get involved with these tiresome Jews and their petty law. Pilate asked Jesus, 'Are you the king of the Jews?' 'You say it,' said Jesus. Pilate said, 'I find no reason to condemn this man.' This upset the temple authorities. The governor found out Jesus was from Galilee, so he sent him to the local ruler, a prince named Herod, but as it was a capital charge Herod sent him back again to the Roman governor, saying it was his responsibility.

The temple priests had now got the mob worked up and they were after blood. Pilate was in a spot. He was already in trouble with Rome, and didn't want any rioting. He tried to get round the mob by offering to set Jesus free to celebrate the Passover. It was traditional to set free a prisoner. But they said, ' Give us Barabbas, and crucify Jesus,' so the mob got its way and so did the temple authorities.

Jesus the carpenter was made to carry his cross to the place of execution, a local rubbish tip. Two common criminals were being put to death at the same time, so there were three crosses on the hillside; Jesus's cross was in the middle. After many hours of suffering, the Roman soldiers broke the legs of the two thieves to finish them off, but when they came to Jesus they found that he was already dead. The N.C.O. in charge stuck his spear into the side of the carpenter, just to make sure.

So it was all over. The man who, from what people were saying, had done so much good, was now dead for crossing the authorities. Now back to the studio.

Chairman: But is it all over? Although the temple police were on guard outside the cave where the body of Jesus was buried, to stop the disciples taking it away, and although the cave was sealed by a large heavy stone, the body disappeared.

The day after the crucifixion was the Jewish Sabbath, so it was the day after that when some women friends of the crucified man came to embalm the body.

Over to Commentator B . . .

[*Slide No. 5*]

2nd Commentator: This is the garden where Jesus was buried; the tomb is just behind me over there. Here is Mary. She came with friends on the Sunday morning. Tell us about it, Mary.

Mary Magdalene: There were three of us. We came to the tomb to embalm the body of our leader and friend Jesus, and to pay our last respects. As we came along the road we were wondering who would roll back the stone from the entrance of the cave, because we knew it was too large for us to move.

But when we got there the stone was rolled away and the body of Jesus gone. We were all very upset; we ran back to our meeting place to tell the men, and some of them came back to have a look.

I was terribly upset. I thought the temple people had taken the body. I wandered off from the tomb but still in this garden, and still weeping. Then I came across someone I thought was the gardener. I asked him if he knew where the body had been taken. He said ' Mary ' and I looked again—and it was Jesus.

2nd Commentator: Are you sure?

Mary Magdalene: As sure as I see you. He told me to go and tell the others, so I did. Some believed what I told them, some didn't. But later that night, while we sat together in our secret meeting place, he came to us.

2nd Commentator: What a strange story, Mary. I am afraid I find it all very unbelievable. Now back to the studio.

Chairman: That is not all, the disciples now say that he has come to them on many occasions, and that as many as 500 of his followers have seen him. Is it a ghost? The disciples say not; they can touch him, and some of his fishermen friends say that he cooked breakfast for them one morning after they had been out fishing.

Where is he now then? Well his followers say he has now gone back to his father in heaven, and that he has promised to send them some hidden power.

What do you make of it all? Was this carpenter from Nazareth the Son of God? Was this God on earth, or are these people deluded or even mad?

In Jewish history there have been many men whom the people thought to be the Messiah. None performed miracles, and all are now forgotten.

I suppose only time will tell if this man Jesus was really the Son of God. If in a few years' time people still speak his name and go on remembering the things he taught, perhaps there may be something in it.

But my guess is that all these events will be forgotten in a week or two.

Good night.

[*Slide No. 6. ' The End '.*]

Taped sound: Programme signature tune.

Voice: ' End of transmission.

Thank you. Great show.'

TAKING PART IN HOLY WEEK

An exciting project worked out in sound and slides by a church group

When the group of 35 lively juniors—more boys than girls—who make up St Dunstan's Guild, Cheam, Surrey, decided that they would like to study the events of Holy Week in real depth, they spent six weeks on research, finding out as much as they could about the biblical story itself and the social and political background against which it took place. Armed with this knowledge, they wrote a script with ten episodes and made a tape recording of this, complete with background music and sound effects.

They also devised a picture sequence of 30 colour slides; this involved a search for appropriate locations and many photographic sessions, all the pictures being taken by one boy. Some of the scenes were most imaginatively conceived, notably the entrance to the tomb, which was suggested by dark clipped yew hedges in a public garden. A real donkey was tracked down and borrowed for the Palm Sunday sequence; regrettably it disgraced itself at one stage by bolting with its rider, but it nevertheless figures in some excellent pictures.

Finally an evening for parents was held at the art gallery where the group usually meets each Sunday and they were able to share in a moving presentation of 'The Events of Holy Week'.

Space unfortunately does not permit us to print the whole script, but an outline of the ten episodes is given below, and may be of interest to other groups who would like to tackle a similar project. Slides are only mentioned if they are of subjects other than the incidents to which the script refers. It is worth noting that the group did not wear costume for the photographs, and this seemed to lead to a greater sense of involvement; they were taking part in something, rather than 'acting'.

The Events of Holy Week
I   Palm Sunday Opening music was Vaughan Williams' Fantasia on a Theme of Thomas Tallis'. A slide of countryside in the Holy Land was accompanied by sounds of approaching donkey's hooves and voices. Jesus asks four of the disciples to bring the donkey which they will find tethered in the nearby village. They are heard

87

to run there, tell the surprised owners that the Master needs the animal, and return with it. Other disciples put their coats on the donkey's back for a saddle. A slide of Jerusalem leads into:

II The Entry into Jerusalem Photographs were accompanied by the noise of a crowd asking questions, then cheering and shouting ' Hosanna! ' The Narrator on the tape pointed out: ' The Elders were worried by the people praising Jesus like this. Jesus himself was sad because he knew that the people did not really understand that he was not a king who would fight for them. He knew that they would soon turn against him. He went with his disciples to the temple.'

III Cleansing the Temple Sounds of buying and selling change to shouts of rage as Jesus tells the stallholders that they are ' abusing this place and the people '. He contrasts them with the blind and sick who come to the temple to pray; listeners hear the crash of overturned tables and the cries of birds. As a blind man begs Jesus to help him in the name of God, one of the sellers begins to see that he has done wrong, and asks for forgiveness and help. The Narrator warns that this incident made the Scribes and Pharisees more determined to get rid of Jesus.

IV The woman who praised Jesus Mark 14. 1–9 in dramatised form.

V The betrayal Brief dialogue between Judas and the Chief Priest, on the theme, ' If you make it worth my while, I will help you to get him.'

VI The Låst Supper Jesus instructs his disciples to follow a man whom they will see carrying a jug of water—he will easily be spotted, even in a crowd, because that is a woman's job. This fades into sounds of a meal in progress. Dialogue is adapted from Mark 14. 18–25.

VII The disciples forsake Jesus: his capture Jesus foretells the disciples' loss of faith and his death and resurrection; Peter loudly denies that he will ever disown Jesus, and all the others agree. Jesus prays in the garden, until the sound of approaching soldiers grows louder. Judas kisses him; there are sounds of fighting; Jesus says, ' All who use the sword die by it as well.... I do not need to fight back against you.'

VIII Trial and Crucifixion ' Mars ' from Holst's *The Planets Suite* and a slide of a house in Jerusalem introduce short readings which describe Peter's betrayal, the examination before the

Sanhedrin, Pilate's acquiescence to the Sanhedrin's demand, and a reading of Mark 15. 25–27, 33–34, 37–39. The music 'Nimrod' from Elgar's *Enigma Variations* leads into:

IX   The Resurrection   Mary Magdalene, Salome and some of the other women are heard approaching. They hear a rumbling like thunder and see that the stone has rolled away from the tomb. After the angel's message, the other women rush away and Mary is left in the garden, where she recognises her Risen Lord. The music breaks into 'Morning' from Grieg's *Peer Gynt Suite*.

X   Jesus appears again   A slide of the Sea of Galilee. The disciples, grumbling about their poor catch, hear a distant voice hailing them: 'Cast your nets on the right side—you'll do better this time!' With great splashing they do so . . . then Peter recognises who has called, and shouts, 'Master—we're coming. . . .'

The Narrator concludes: 'So Jesus showed his disciples that he had overcome the cross and had risen from the dead. His work on earth was finished. But he left them not only with his example to follow, but also with instructions to carry on his teaching, saying, " Lo, I am with you always, even unto the end of the world ".'

The last slides were pictures of the 35 Guild members themselves with their families—a part of his Church today.

AN EASTER MIME WITH MUSIC

Sally Rosina Houghton's Sunday school worked out their own version of the Easter story

The children of the Sunday school at Newton, near Tewkesbury, decided that an Easter mime would be rather more unusual to produce than a play done at Christmas.

The elder class elected to be in charge. There were twelve in this class, with an age range of 7–12. The eldest boy became thoroughly absorbed as ' producer ' and we gained many pleasant ideas as the children all began to take an active part.

Sunday school is held in the building of a residential nursery. It is a large house with spacious rooms and we are lucky in being able to use the main hall. There is a lot of woodwork and a large sweeping staircase which sets off the stained-glass windows and makes an ideal setting for many plays, because we are able to act on various planes and the action can take place *in* the audience, too (see diagram).

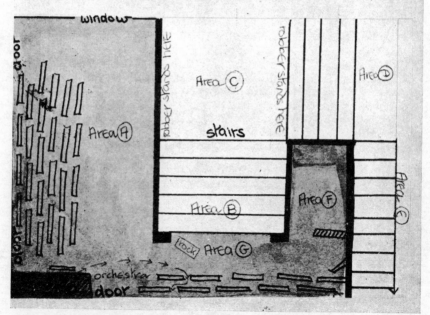

A Plan of The Hall (showing where action takes place)

No dressing up

The setting was, in this case, abstract. We did not use a backcloth, neither did we ' dress up '.

Children always thoroughly enjoy dressing up. When asked if they would like to do so this time, the immediate reaction was a unanimous ' yes '. But, looking at the calendar, I realised that the performance was only four weeks away. I felt that the aim should be a good performance in everyday clothes, rather than a rather second-rate one in shoddy costumes. The children agreed, and we felt that, as the play was abstract and rather modern, having no costumes would be advantageous. For example, one little boy acted the rock which guarded the tomb. He is physically handicapped and cannot walk. The children felt that it was a good idea for him to sit on his tricycle as ' the rock '. In our abstract setting this seemed perfectly acceptable, although it might not have done so on a stage and in costume.

The fact that no one was in costume also made the ' orchestra ' seem a real part of the play. Everyone was equal.

The ' orchestra ' consisted of three girls and myself. We acted on our own judgment—ad lib. Rarely did I know what strange noise would issue forth next! At the beginning of the work all of the children were enchanted by the instruments, all wanting to hit, slosh and sing. Order was restored and three recorder players chosen.

Speaking parts were mainly represented by instruments (see pictures). Apart from those instruments shown, we also used the piano. Various ' clashing ' notes, accompanied by voices, represented the wailing relatives and friends of the three on the crosses.

Children's choice

The voice was used to add a personal note to music, e.g. while the angels descended from heaven (i.e. came downstairs), one little girl sang ' There is a green hill '. ' Poor Jenny is a-weeping ' was suggested by the children and this was hummed as Mary, walking in the garden, found the rock rolled away. The humming was interrupted as Mary touched the rock—a great gasp rent the air, to show her reaction. At the end of the play the little ones (about 15 of them, aged up to seven) descended from heaven as angels singing ' Jesus loves me '. (The last line was changed, by request, to ' he died to save us all '. The children suggested that this gave a better final impression and I wholeheartedly agreed, feeling ' the Bible tells me so ' to be unsuitable.)

We realised that it would be controversial to have the robbers descend as angels. We all discussed it, and decided that this would show how they had been forgiven.

The action of the play	Instruments

(Before the play begins, the little ones are installed upstairs in Area E, as angels.)

A solemn procession — Jesus, robbers, soldiers, mourners—enters Area A, and slowly makes its way up the first part of the stairs, Area B. The mourners kneel and lie about the foot of the stairs. The two robbers stand parallel to each other on the stairs (see diagram). Jesus faces down the stairs. **Drums**
Roman soldiers are hustling the crowd and keeping them back. **Gong, cymbals**
A loud stroke on the gong marks the **Gong**
moment when nailing begins, carried out **Triangles**
by the first Roman soldier.
Another loud stroke on the gong heralds **Gong**
Jesus' words (spoken):

Jesus: Father, forgive them.
His head falls forward as he dies.
Music from the tubular chimes symbolises
goodness and purity. **Tubular chimes**
Immediately wailing begins, as the soldiers **Piano and voices**
remove the body of Jesus. (It was decided **singing and**
that the soldiers should help Joseph of **speaking**
Arimathaea to carry the body to the cave, as
after the first rehearsal several large splinters
had to be removed after it was dragged to
the tomb.) Joseph leaves. Wailing stops.
Rock rolled before tomb.
First Roman soldier talks to the second **Voices speaking**
about the behaviour of the crucified men as
they go upstairs to Area C. They remove
robbers and go on upstairs to Area D. Deep
music on piano suggests earth and burial. **Piano**
Robbers continue upstairs to high piano
music suggesting forgiveness, joy and
Paradise.
Roman soldiers descend from Area D,
chatting about other crimes and criminals **Voices speaking**
to be dealt with, part, and exit.

Hymn: ' There is a green hill ' **Solo singing voice**

The two robbers (who are now angels) descend during the hymn and roll away

the rock from the tomb. Jesus bounds upstairs to Area D.

The angels wait in the tomb for Mary, who
enters Area A, sobbing. As she enters,
voices hum ('Poor Jenny is a-weeping'.)
When she sees the rock at Area G, she
touches it, throws back her arms and gasps
(aided by loud gasps from the orchestra,
who interrupt their humming).

Voices humming

Angels: Why are you weeping?

Mary: Because they have taken Jesus
away and I do not know where they have
laid him. (Mary sobs, Jesus descends the
stairs and stands before her.)

Humming resumes

Jesus: Why are you weeping?

Mary: Because they have taken Jesus
away. (Jesus holds out his hands to her as
she kneels.)

Jesus: Mary!
She lays her hands on his and looks into his
face.

Mary: Jesus!
It is now that the younger ones descend the
stairs from Area E. Bounding along, flap-
ping rather than fluttering their outstretched
arms (wings), they sing 'Jesus loves me'.
Beaming, they encircle Jesus and Mary on
the stairs at Areas B and C.

Voices singing, with
piano, tubular
chimes and cymbals

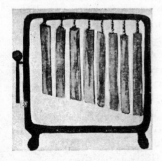

Tubular chimes have a very
pleasing sound — clear and
high. They can be used to
convey a feeling of goodness
and purity, of good overcoming
evil

The throbbing rhythm of
the large gong suggests
an air of urgency. The
gong can provide you with
quiet noises as well as
with ear-splitting crashes
(which, incidentally, serve
well as cues). It also gives
the impression of a large,
murmuring crowd

A cymbal adds to
the noise of the
crowd, and sug-
gests a sharp, bitter
feeling in the air

Two interlinked triangles, hit re-
peatedly, are suitable for use at
the nailing to the cross

Home-made drums have a dull,
vibrating voice, and when hit
with the palm of the hand they
serve well to give a feeling of a
large, approaching crowd. This
drum, which is about two feet
high, can be made from an
empty oil drum which is made
hollow at each end. A circle of
tractor inner-tube is stretched
over the hollow cylinder and kept
in place with string. Smaller
drums can be similarly made,
using tins. The instruments
should be gaily painted

EMMAUS

A poem by D. M. Bates which catches something of the joy and certainty of the Resurrection experience

We fled the city and began to walk
Out in the dust and heat,
Fearful of danger, and with bitter talk
Urged the unwilling feet.
Till the lone traveller joined us as we sped.
' Going your way,' he said.

We scarce looked up to see the friendly smile,
Until he asked us why.
' Where had he been ? Had he not heard the trial,
Nor seen the prophet die ?
We could not yet believe it was the end—
He was our greatest friend.'

And then the stranger talked. He knew it all—
Scripture and history.
Explained it, line by line, from our first fall,
To this last mystery;
Till the long miles to our own house-door led.
' You must come in,' we said.

We lit familiar candles in the gloom;
Everything looked the same.
Laid supper for the stranger in the room—
We did not know his name
Till we sat down and heard the prayer he said,
And saw him break the bread.

Oh life unquenchable! Oh friend unknown!
All the time it was you.
On the long journey we were not alone,
Now we know that it's true:
Nothing is lost; home or away, you are near—
You are alive! You are here!

ALONG THE NATURE TRAIL

Trevor Kerry suggests a starting point relevant to the season of Easter

Most syllabuses of religious education make some provision for teaching about Creation. Happily, the vast majority have progressed beyond setting Genesis 1 as a set text for juniors! However, whether the course does this or explores creation themes that are available from the child's experience, the aim must remain the same as this age: to impart a sense of mystery and wonder at the fact of *life*. Creation, spring-time and Easter belong together and the latter season is the time to be thinking about ways of exploring this mystery of life in the natural world.

There is no lack of stimuli:

a baby brother or sister born to the pupil's family;
the words of a hymn (*English Hymnal* 299, 587 etc);
a large picture or wallchart;
a cageful of white mice;
a birdtable outside the window;
a record of bird sound ('Bird Sounds in Close-Up', MAL 1102);
a Teacher's Pack from the Royal Society for the Protection of Birds (The Lodge, Sandy, Beds).

One exciting possibility has been omitted from the list: the visit to a nature trail or wildfowl reserve. There can be no better activity as a starter or follow-up, and for many children the concentration of so many colourful and unusual creatures in so small an area is a genuine adventure. Of course, the idea may seem impractical at first; but most areas have a local Naturalists' Trust which will provide details of local facilities. Try the telephone directory or consult the Local Education Authority. Those within reach of such reserves as Slimbridge or Peakirk, made famous by Peter Scott, will find available facilities for picnics and for viewing even in bad weather; and the number of private reserves is on the increase.

The basic pattern of most reserves or trails is to provide a walk along which are a series of marked and numbered posts. Each post denotes a spot where you are likely to find a bird, flower etc. of special interest, and a leaflet gives details of the main attractions at each post. If, then, a properly managed trail is really inaccessible, why not make your own? Even in the heart of major cities many churches still have churchyards which hold a host of wild creatures: squirrels straying from a nearby park, greenfinches in the fir-trees, woodlice under a rotting log, or a thrush's anvil surrounded by the shells of its victims.

Even if you can't go outdoors a trail is still possible. Turn the church hall into a nature reserve! You can have pictures on the walls, a display of suitable books, a projector set up showing slides in a shady corner. The RSPB sell very realistic cardboard models of birds which can be painted and hung from the ceiling; or you can make animal tracks from card cut to shape and placed on the floors for people to follow from one display to another. Let the children write a trail guide, and make up quizzes for others to try.

There is no shortage of ideas when you start a theme from nature. Increasing awareness of, and concern for, living creatures will result; as well as a new store of knowledge for the children about the world in which they live, and a sense of many questions still unanswered. The sense of mystery and the desire to express thanksgiving and worship will be very much alive. And you can take courage from the fact that even St Paul recommended this approach as a road to God: ' He has made himself known to all men everywhere through the world which he has made; this is plain for all men to see. . . . As we learn what a man is like from the things he has made, so we can learn what God is like from what God has made ' (Romans 1. 19, 20. *New World*, OUP).

THE DEAD STICK

A springtime story for the youngest
by Ivy Russell

The Brown family had moved to another town, and when Peter started at his new school he found himself sitting beside a boy called Brad (short for Bradley).

Peter wasn't sure if he liked Brad very much, but one thing was certain. Brad was big and clever, and the other boys were a bit scared of him. So Peter felt flattered when Brad began to talk to him.

'I'm going to look for newts down in the pool on Sunday morning,' said Brad. 'Want to come?'

Peter hesitated.

'I'd like to but—there's Sunday school,' he began.

Brad gasped, and his eyes opened wide.

'Sunday school?' he repeated. 'You don't believe all that stuff about the Bible, do you? Miracles and all that? You must be crazy!'

'Well, I only go because my mum makes me,' said Peter hastily. 'But—I'll come to the pool this week instead.' So instead of going to Sunday school he crept off in the other direction. As he left the garden he stopped at an old bush and broke off a dead stick to swish about, as Brad always did. They poked about in the pool all morning, and Peter knew he ought to be feeling clever and important—only he wasn't. He felt terribly guilty, and he hoped nobody would see him.

When he got home he hastily poked the stick in a corner near the front door, and forgot all about it.

To Peter's relief, Brad was moved into another class soon after, and their friendship fizzled out. But one thing remained. Peter kept remembering Brad's scoffing words, 'You don't believe all that stuff about the Bible, do you? Miracles and all that? You must be crazy!' Peter couldn't find the right answer, and he grew more and more miserable.

Spring came in with soft winds and blue skies, and father was out in the garden at every opportunity. One day he called excitedly to the family:

'Come and see! We've got a lovely new fuchsia bush growing by the front door!'

They all hurried out, and to Peter's amazement, there was his old dry stick with dozens of leafy shoots springing up all around.

' But it can't be alive! That was a dead stick! ' he gasped.

' It's just another miracle,' said father. ' In springtime there are so many going on all around that we quite lose count. The first Easter Day was the biggest miracle of all, but it wasn't the last, by any means.'

It seemed to Peter that the sun had suddenly burst out from behind a cloud. What did Brad know about it, anyway? He'd never even read the Bible!

TWICE IN A PASCHAL MOON

Daphne Llewellyn discovers that happy coincidences can occur on Easter holiday courses

' This is the best holiday course we have ever had ! ' We have said this on many occasions, so perhaps we were biased this time by the fact that we, as official leaders and helpers, learned and gained more than ever from the events of Holy Week. We were assured that school holidays and Holy Week coincided only once in a paschal moon, so had begun our planning with a creation course on earth, air, fire and water, with emphasis on simplicity of living, to enjoy and thank God for the gifts of creation. Ideas came thick and fast and when we discovered that this coincidence *could* happen twice in a paschal moon we didn't want to waste them. They had to be incorporated into something that would lead up to a service suitable for the remembrance of the Crucifixion and Resurrection. So a framework was born:

Monday	God gives us himself in the world
Tuesday	God gives himself in our families
Wednesday	God gives himself in other people—in a world family
Thursday	God gives himself on the cross

Monday went well according to plan. We borrowed apparatus from a local school to investigate air and water, watched tadpoles, started a seed germinator going, smashed open stones to see how beautiful they were inside, made candles and a garden of Eden, lit a bonfire and did many other things that filled us with joy and wonder at God's created world and established a longing to care for it as he would wish us to. We learnt a riddle song about creation and I listened to another about an amoeba and then we played an amoeba game, finding that our groups grew by gobbling up existing groups and then splitting up in different ways as the group became too large.

On Tuesday we played games that helped us to understand our need for each other and how impossible it was to do things entirely on our own. We told and re-enacted the story of Noah and how

100

he was called with his family into the confines of the ark and after the storm went out to people the world with new hope that mankind would be less evil. Then we erected tents and started family groups, some caring for pets, some playing ' house ', some modelling different types of houses to be built into a town next day.

So far all had gone according to plan. Then something quite spontaneous happened. The group in the larger tent started to sing and children from other tents left their own ' homes ' to join in. The course had taken the direction we had planned, but a day too soon. From then on teachers became pupils in a very real sense. We racked our brains at that afternoon's planning meeting for another way to make the family groups need each other.

The amoeba experience

Next morning found us depleted in staff and with a sudden influx of many more younger children. Our carefully laid plans were useless. Result—panic, chaos. What should we do? We felt as though we were completely gobbled up by the amoeba. We were miserable and helpless. Then there was an explosion into new and smaller groups. All sorts of things began to happen in the groups—a lively dance to the music from *Noye's Fludde*, pictures drawn with charcoal from the bonfire, the older boys showing the younger ones how to draw pictures on squared paper. Suddenly we found we were hastening to serve groups with the things they needed.

Everyone had something to do and something they had chosen for themselves. In the midst of it all there was time to talk for really long periods to many of the children and to exchange their ideas with our own. Towards the end of the morning some of us made a great noise with trumpets and percussion instruments, and everyone came running from their small groups into one huge one on the grass at the back of the church. Here we sang ' Happy Birthday ' to one of our number and shared a birthday cake, made in the shape of a cross, in a glorious *agape*, which reminded us of the celebrations of the early Christians.

On Thursday we remembered how God had given himself on the cross and, because we would not all meet together on Easter Day, linked it with the resurrection. We acted out life-cycles of bulbs and seeds with the younger children. The older ones worked out mimes to show how so many things have to be destroyed to build something new that is fine and good. In discussion we linked this with Jesus' death on the cross to show us a new way of life—a new stage in evolution. The new way hadn't come when God destroyed the world in Noah's time. He had to come into the world and be part of it and to die in order to show us a new way of life.

Then we painted and modelled symbols of Good Friday and Easter to reinforce our ideas.

On Friday we gathered with the parents for worship together in church. We could not share our own learning and experience, for that will never be the same the second time round. Instead we endeavoured to recreate a new experience based on our own learning. We invited everyone to look, to listen, to love and to lay themselves open so that God could give us all a new message on that day. In an endeavour to recreate the chaos and disillusion of the first Good Friday we again played the amoeba game. It resulted in many of us finding ourselves in a different seat in the church—some of us even reduced to sitting on the floor. We found, too, that we had a new leader. After the chaos the children asked us to make waves for their Noah's ark and later they acted out experiences of death and resurrection for us. Whilst all this was going on, hot cross buns were cooking in the oven back at the Centre. The service ended with a procession of the cooks carrying the buns, and a blessing of the buns and distribution to all in Church.

We are grateful to all who shared in the activity with us and to those who have told us of their growing understanding of the amoeba experience. We thank particularly the Vicar for the way in which he so sensitively responded to the needs of all of us in his opening and closing remarks.

We used *Winding Quest* (OUP), Alan Dale's adaptation of Old Testament stories for schools, for biblical material on the course. The language is truly beautiful and we heartily recommend it to interested parents.

GEORGE AND THE DRAGON

The dragon is befriended by George in this play devised by a junior church group in Eastbourne and transcribed by John Davey

SCENE ONE

[A park in the middle of a large town. An old lady is sitting on a bench with a shopping bag beside her. Enter a group of children]

George: This will be a good place to try out my kite.

Jill: It's not very windy—do you think it will fly?

George: 'Course it will.

Old lady: Be careful with that thing, children—do you hear me?
[The kite lifts off the ground and slowly rises. It soon comes down again and as it goes so, knocks the old lady's hat from her head. The children make no attempt to pick it up and begin a game of tag with a great deal of whooping and shouting].

Old Lady: Go away and play somewhere else, you noisy horrid children! Go away at *once!*

George: Go away yourself, you old dragon.
[Exit Old Lady. The children continue their game]

John: That was Mrs Burns. She lives in the Old People's Home. She always stops here for a bit of a sit-down on her way back from the shops.

George: I don't care who she is, miserable old thing. Shouting at us like that—We didn't do her any harm . . . only knocked her silly old hat off . . . *[laughs].* 'Bye—see you tomorrow.
[Exit children]

103

SCENE TWO: Next day

[*Enter children, now dressed as cowboys and Indians*]

George: There's that old girl again—come on, let's capture her!

[*Enter Old Lady, moving with great difficulty and carrying a heavy shopping basket.*

The children move stealthily towards her. George lets off a barrage of shots from cap pistols. She, startled, moves off stage hurriedly.]

Jill: You shouldn't have done that, George. You might have given her a heart attack.

George: Good riddance, I say . . . she can't even walk properly— look at her. [*He imitates the Old Lady's walk. The other children continue their game but their attitude towards George seems to change. He is left out rather pointedly.*

Exit George. On his way offstage he calls out, ' 'Bye!' No one answers.

Exit other children in opposite direction.]

SCENE THREE: Next day

[*Enter children, and George from opposite direction*]

George: Hullo. Where's the old lady today?

Jill: Don't know.

John: I expect she's dead. You must have given her an awful fright yesterday. [*He turns away and joins the other children, who are playing ' Ambulances '*]

George: Can I play?

John: You wouldn't be any good at making people better— You'd give 'em all heart attacks.

George: Is she really dead?

Jill: I didn't see Mrs Burns at the shops—did you, John?

John: No, Her milk was still outside when I delivered the paper this morning. She always takes her milk in first thing. [*He pauses dramatically—making the most of George's discomfort. The other children gather round*]

George: Shouldn't we go round and see?

John: You can if you like. I wouldn't dare. Suppose the police are waiting for the murderer!

Jill: You go, George. [*The other children join in:* 'Go on, bet you're scared.']

George: I'm not scared. [*Frightened of losing face, he turns to John*]. Where did you say Mrs Burns lives?

John: At the Old People's Home in our road.
[*Exit George, the other children following*]

SCENE FOUR: Same day. Outside Mrs Burns' flat.
[*George is knocking, first softly and then, after no reply, more loudly*]

George: Anybody there?

Old Lady: [*faintly*] Who's there? What do you want?

George: It's George Simpson, are you all right?

Old Lady: Come in—the door's on the latch.
[*George, John and Jill enter to find Mrs Burns sitting in a chair*]

John: Are you all right, Mrs Burns?

Old Lady: You're Mrs Jones' little boy, aren't you? I've hurt my back. I think I've strained it. Can you fetch the doctor?

George: I'll go, Mrs Burns.
[*Exit George, looking very important*]

John: Can I make you a cup of tea?

Old Lady: That would be nice. Thank you.

Jill: I'll help, John.
[*Enter George, accompanied by Doctor*]

Doctor: What have you been up to, Mrs Burns?
[*Low conversation between doctor and Mrs Burns. He turns to the children*] 'You can be of great help if you can do Mrs Burns' shopping for her for the next few days. She isn't badly hurt, but she'll have to stay in bed for a while.

George: I will, doctor.

Old Lady: Thank you, dearie. You're a proper St George! Here is a list of things I need, the money's in the purse.
[*Exit George with shopping basket. The other children waiting outside, cluster round George as he moves offstage*]

105

ROUND THE FIELDS
ON ROGATION DAY

To 'townies' in a Newcastle church Rogation meant little—until Joyce Gray and her teachers arranged an outing with a purpose

It was a summer camp in the country which first inspired the idea. The Rector of Wycliffe, near Castle Barnard, where our Guide company was spending a week, suggested that the following year we should bring a party of children from our church to join his parish at their Rogationtide service.

To city dwellers, the festival of Rogationtide means little. I know from my own childhood experience that this is true. As I grew up in the Anglican Church it was a meaningless word to me: I vaguely knew that it had something to do with planting the crops but that was all. I knew, therefore, that this would be very true of the youngsters in our Sunday schools, and probably of our group leaders (as we call the teenage teachers) also. For all of us, a Rogation Sunday outing into the country would be an education in the truest sense of the word.

We planned our project well in advance, so that it could begin two weeks before Rogation Sunday itself, and also in order that coaches could be booked. A letter was sent to all parents of junior children, explaining carefully that this was to be a Sunday school outing with a purpose. The response was tremendous: 128 children brought back permission forms, and we realised that with group leaders we would be a party of over 140 people. The Rector of Wycliffe did not seem daunted by these numbers, however, and so preparations went ahead.

Week 1 During the first Sunday session, we practised the hymns on the Order of Service which the Rector had sent us. The group leader's task was to familiarise the children in their group with the word ' Rogation ': the children were taught that it means ' asking ', and is the time when we seek God's blessing on the crops and work of the countryside. (We knew that industry should be included, but decided that it was not appropriate in this particular project.) We tried to convey to the children that man works the land in full co-operation with God, and that at this time he acknowledges his dependence upon God for the growth ' from seed time unto harvest '.

Week 2 Again we practised the hymns together, and then dispersed to the various groups. This week the group leaders described the places where the procession would go: from a service in the tiny church to the village green, a meadow, a river, a cornfield, a farmyard, a garden and finally back to the churchyard. Instruction sheets, to tell parents exactly where the children should meet, what they should take and their likely time of return, were issued to be taken home.

Week 3 The great day! Three coaches took us all to Wycliffe in the morning, and the children spent a blissful hour playing in the natural paddling pool made at one point by the river. At 2.30 everyone packed into the tiny church: there were children round the font, up the aisle and in the sanctuary, but they were in! The first part of the service consisted of a hymn, address (an excellent, short one from a visiting preacher who was a training college tutor) and bidding prayers; then the lengthy procession began, visiting all the places described to the children beforehand, and ending with the blessing in the church. After a picnic tea, the coaches took us all to the village hall for a hot drink before the journey home.

As well as a teaching day—and all of us ' townies ', adults and children alike, will in future have a much greater understanding of Rogationtide—it was a valuable day so far as relationships were concerned. The day of happiness which they spent with each other and with older Christian people will be stored in their minds and be connected with church life. And how important it is that experience within the church in childhood should be pleasurable!

FIRE! FIRE!

A service for Whitsun, by D. J. Bartlett and the teachers and children of St Leonard's junior Sunday school, Wollaton, Notts.

(The words of the hymn ' Thank you for all the warmth of sunshine ' were put together by the Rev. D. J. Bartlett on the basis of ideas and suggestions written down by the junior children; verse 4 was written entirely by a nine-year old girl. The tune is that of ' Thank you for every new good morning ', to be found in several collections of modern hymns, including *Youth Praise* (Falcon Press). The words of ' The Lord, the Giver of Life,' were composed by members of a Sunday school teachers' conference, and the tune is Mr Bartlett's own composition. The children's prayers and poems are included as examples only; your group will, of course, use its own work!)

Hymn: Praise, my soul, the King of heaven.'
[*All remain standing.*]

Introduction: We have come here today to worship God; to give thanks for his great gift of fire, and to ask that his Spirit may fill us, as he filled the first Christians, with great strength and power.

Prayer [*said together*]: O God, accept the praise we offer;
guide our thoughts
that we may learn more about you,
and that we may feel your power
in our lives. Amen.

[*All sit. The Conductor gives a brief explanation of the theme and the way in which it will be explored during the service. At St Leonard's this was followed by a dance drama by children from a local school, on ' The Discovery of Fire '.*]

Song [*sung by all, twice through*]: ' London's burning! '

Thoughts on fire and its uses

A reader: Clang goes the bell of the fire-engine;
Crackling, flaming, the house comes down,
The terrible smell of tyres on the car.
A cascade of flames come showering out;
Then the flames spring up as the water touches—
They dance the dance of the fire.
The fire slowly smoulders,
And all that is left is cinders and ruins.

Speaker A: Yes, fire can be dangerous; it can burn down your house; it can burn down great buildings; in the great fire of London, a large part of the city was destroyed.

Speaker B: In a forest fire, millions of trees can be burned down. People may be killed in a fire; people are often injured and burnt.

Speaker C: Fire can be a burning furnace of smoke and flames; something meaning destruction to all nature, to all God's creation, great and small. Fire is a thing of terror when it gets out of hand.

A: But fire also gives us warmth in cold weather, whether it is a nice cosy home fire to sit by, or a boiler to warm the radiator.

B: When snow is falling, I sit and say to myself how lucky I am to be warm and snug.

C: This brings us much comfort, and helps us to keep healthy and to get rid of our colds.

A: Fire also gives us light to see by, whether it is the light of the sun, or from electric light.

B: It is by the light of fire that we can see and enjoy beautiful colours.

C: It is the heat of the fiery sun which warms the earth and helps things to grow. Without the heat of fire, there would be no life at all.

A: By the heat of fire we cook our food, and can have hot food and drink.

B: Fire gives us pleasure; it is soothing; it means 'welcome'— again as a home-fire to sit by, or as a camp-fire or bonfire on Bonfire Night to be merry at, with fireworks and potatoes baked in their jackets.

Poem [*read by the child who wrote it*]:
Standing by the bonfire,
What a lovely sight—
All the flames are colourful
As they glare in the night.
The flames are yellow, orange, red:
They jump and frisk all about.
They look so very pretty
Until the fire is out.

A: What a wonderful thing fire is:

B: And how necessary it is to our whole existence.

C: How man must have rejoiced when he discovered fire and found that he could make use of it.

[*At St Leonard's, here followed another dance drama, ' Fire for power'.*]

Prayers of Thanks for Fire

A: Lord God, for giving us fire to keep us warm in the cold:

Response [*by all, after each sentence*]*:* We thank you, God.

B: For the sun, which sends down its golden rays to make us warm, and which brightens the garden:

A: For the light by which we are able to see:

B: For our food which is cooked by fire:

A: For our hot water, heated by the fire:

B: For the pleasures and cosiness of fire:

A: For cars and for all forms of transport which we ride in:

B: For coal for fires, and for the coalman who brings us coal faithfully when we are in need of it:

A: For Mummy, who keeps our home fire under control:

B: For firemen, who rescue people from burning buildings:

A: For the ambulance men, who hurry injured people to hospital:

B: For doctors and nurses, who tend us in hospital when we are burnt:

Response: We thank you, God.

The Conductor: And we will pray for safety from the dangers of fire:

Prayer [*read by child who wrote it*]:
O God, please bless all firemen,
who have to get up on cold winter nights
to put out fires;
and bless them when they are fighting a fire:
and help us not to be silly
or do dangerous things with fire,
because we may get burnt
or cause someone else to be burnt:
through Jesus Christ our Lord. Amen.

Hymn: Thank you for all the warmth of sunshine,
Thank you for its bright golden rays;
Thank you for all the joy it brings
    On sunny summer days.

Thank you for fire which keeps us warm, Lord;
Thank you for fire which gives us light;
Thank you for all the lovely colours
    And the gift of sight.

Thank you for all the coal beneath us;
Thank you for gas and oil and wood;
Thank you for ovens and for stoves
    On which we cook our food.

Thank you for all the warmth and comfort;
Thank you for all our fires so bright;
Thank you for all the joy of fireworks
    Every bonfire night.

Thank you for every kind of transport;
Thank you for power which makes things go;
Thank you for all machines which help our
    Living here below.

Thank you for all the helpful firemen;
Thank you for all the lives they save;
Bless them, and teach us when there's fire
    How best we should behave.

[*All sit. This could be the place for an Address, but at St Leonard's the following dialogue was used:*]

Fire and the Spirit of God

A: Fire gives warmth. Warmth. Warmth is something which we need in our hearts too—

B: —the warmth of joy and happiness:

111

C: the warmth of feeling secure and safe:

B: the warmth of knowing that we are at one with other people.

A: This is the warmth given us by the Spirit of God.

B: This is God in our hearts, warming us up:

C: Our own form of central heating, or an open fire in our hearth.

A: If we have this warmth, then we shall be warm towards others:

B: we shall be warm-hearted: we will show the warmth of friendship:

C: we shall attract others by the warmth of our love and concern.

ALL: The Spirit of God gives warmth.

A: Fire, once it has caught, spreads amazingly. Fire spreads.

B: So does warm-heartedness, the warmth of love, the warmth of God's Spirit.

C: It will spread far and wide if we give it the chance by being warm-hearted to others.

A: This is the Spirit of God being passed on from person to person—

B: —as a forest fire spreads from tree to tree—

C: —or as a town fire spreads from building to building.

ALL: The Spirit of God, once it has caught, spreads amazingly like wildfire.

A: Fire gives power. Power.

B: Power makes things go.

A: And power is something we need in our lives, too: inner power.

C: Power to do hard and difficult things:

B: —power to be warm-hearted:

C: —power to help spread the love and knowledge of God:

B: —power to make us go.

A: This is the power of God's Spirit within us.

C: —like an engine inside us making us go in the way we are meant to.

B: —keeping us on the move.

ALL: The Spirit of God gives power.

A: The work of God in the world is to give warmth:

B: —to spread his love and knowledge of him:

C: —and to give power.

ALL: Warmth—spreading—power.

A: Perhaps that is why fire has always been used as a symbol of the Spirit of God active among men.

B: Moses felt that he met God in a burning bush, a bush which seemed to be ablaze but was not consumed.

C: The Israelites believed that God led them through the wilderness in a column of fire.

B: One of the psalm writers described his feelings towards God as like a fire within him.

C: John the Baptist said that the Christ would baptise ' with the fire of the Holy Spirit '.

A: And on the first Whit Sunday, when the Spirit of God came with great power upon the Apostles, it was as though. . . .

B: . . . . tongues of fire appeared, and rested upon each one of them,

C: . . . and they were all filled with the Spirit of God and began to speak in tongues, as the Spirit gave them power to proclaim the gospel.

A: Let us hear, then, the story of that first Whit Sunday—

ALL: The gift of the Holy Spirit.

[*Here followed a two-scene dramatic presentation ' The gift of the Holy Spirit ' from ' A Man Called Jesus ' by J. B. Phillips, published by Fontana. A reading could be substituted, perhaps accompanied by mime. Between the two scenes, all stood to sing the hymn below.*]

Hymn: There's a fire in the heart of man,
    There's a warmth in the power of the sun;
    There's a flame that's bright making darkness light,
    That abundant life may come.
        There's fire in the gift of the Spirit,
        The Lord, the Giver of Life.

Now energy's the power we use
To walk and run and play,
To move turbines, ships and trains and cars,
And strong enough to move the stars.
> There's energy in the gift of the Spirit,
> The Lord, the Giver of Life.

There's a pull in the tide and the earth;
There are secret forces and powers;
The wires and the winds and the unseen rays
Are for us and their use is ours.
> There's unseen power in the Spirit,
> The Lord, the Giver of Life.

We learn and read of famous people.
Who've helped us as they could;
Their skills are part of God's Creation
To influence us for good.
> There's love in the gift of the Spirit,
> The Lord, the Giver of Life.

The disciples had been sad and lonely,
Like sheep who had gone astray;
But then one day the Spirit came
And set them on a bold new Way.
> There's boldness in the gift of the Spirit,
> The Lord, the Giver of Life.

[*Here followed a dance drama to the spiritual ' Kum-ba-yah ', sung by all.*]

Prayer [*said together*]: O God, who has given us fire to warm us:
make me like a little fire,
always bright and cheerful,
and warming all who come near me.
Make my soul like a flame pure and clear,
shining in the darkness for all to see. Amen.

The Lord's Prayer.

Hymn: ' Come down, O love divine.'

The Blessing.

IN SEARCH OF THE SPIRIT

John Nettleship suggests ways of tackling 'the most difficult lesson'

A Sunday school teacher admitted to me recently that she thought the most difficult lesson of the year to teach was that on Whit Sunday. 'How can one expect children to understand what is meant by the Holy Spirit?' she asked. I believe that this is a difficulty shared by many teachers. At Christmas we can point to the stable and the star and the child Jesus, at Easter to a tangible cross, an empty tomb and a Risen Christ. In most of our teaching we are able to fix the attention of our scholars upon something concrete—and let us not forget that a child's thinking is generally in concrete, not abstract terms. Hence the difficulty of conveying to them an idea such as that of the Holy Spirit. Added to this is the fact that probably our own thinking on the subject is not too clear!

Here are one or two simple illustrations which may help teachers to clarify their own thinking, and to make this rather difficult doctrine understandable to children. In no sense are the illustrations which follow perfect analogies—they are merely suggestive of certain truths.

First of all, there are the physical symbols associated with Pentecost—the rushing mighty wind, and the tongues of fire. Notice that the Bible says ' a sound *as* of a rushing mighty wind ' and ' tongues like *as* fire '. The writer was surely trying to express the inexpressible. There are some experiences for which ordinary language is quite inadequate—that is why we have poets! Some of the things which poets say may not bear a very logical examination, or really make sense when you look at them coldly and dispassionately; but the fact remains that they express and convey the poet's feelings. A rapturous mother may hug her baby and say, ' I could eat you! ' We all know that she could not; but we also know what she means. And the men and women who had a great experience at Pentecost could not find ordinary words in which to express their feelings; haltingly they said, ' It was as though ... as though ... Oh, as though a great wind swept through us, cleansing us from all that was unclean, and as though a great flame of love burned inside us.'

Or, it may help to discover, through discussion and experiment,

115

that there are many real things in the world which *cannot be seen*—wireless waves, invisible electricity, the wind.

> ' Who has seen the wind?
> Neither you nor I.
> But when the trees bow down their heads.
> The wind is passing by.'

We do not see the wind, but we see its effects. So too at Pentecost; the Holy Spirit himself was invisible, but the *effect* of his influence was very clear—the great change, for example, in the disciples themselves. They became different, braver, purer, more joyful, more able people. They received power—as Jesus promised they would—and that power sent them out unafraid into a hostile world.

And what was this power? Notice, we have already spoken of ' himself ' and ' his '. We must avoid any idea of a vague impersonal influence. What happened to the disciples was the result of God himself at work in them. We say, ' they were filled with the Spirit '. This means that something of God himself actually entered into them. If children find this idea difficult to follow, we may show how something of the kind can happen on a purely human level. We talk of a leader of men, or the captain of a team, ' filling his men with something of his own spirit '. Is it not just as if some essential quality of personality is transferred in this way from one person to another? Through the influence of a vigorous personality, weak men may become strong, cowardly men brave, indifferent men enthusiastic. If human personality can achieve this, how much more can be wrought when the Spirit of God touches men's hearts?

The writer realises that these suggestions over-simplify what is a profound spiritual experience. All our theology is an attempt to explain experience. The doctrine of the Holy Spirit is men's halting attempt to explain the transcendent experience of Pentecost. which has been repeated in the hearts of believing men and women ever since.

We cannot teach children about the Holy Spirit in the way that we can teach them the names of the twelve disciples. We can but try reverently to tell of the experience of godly men and women in every generation. We hope that in those to whom we talk there will awake the response of faith and expectancy which will enable them, in due season, to receive whatever gifts of the Spirit are given.

'A STRONG WIND IN JERUSALEM'

A 'television script' devised by a junior group from New Malden and their teacher, John Brown

Characters:
TV Announcer, ' Israel TV '.
Rachel Cohen, TV Interviewer.
1st and 2nd Bystanders.
Miriam, a domestic servant.
Peter, a disciple.
Priest.

TV Announcer: [*seated at news desk in studio*]: Good evening. This is Israel Television with News at Nine. There have been large demonstrations today in the Old Market Square of Jerusalem. They began, quite unexpectedly, at about 8 a.m. and lasted for most of the day. At one time there were crowds of nearly 5,000 people in and around the square.

The demonstrations were started by a small group of people, followers of the Galilean preacher called Jesus who was executed by the authorities only a few weeks previous, and said by his followers to have risen from the dead. The reason for these disturbances is still far from clear. Their effect, however, has been considerable. Over 3,000 people have today become followers of Jesus. For a fuller report on the day's events we go over now to our reporter on the spot, Rachel Cohen.

R. Cohen: [*Standing in the Old Market Square*]: Good evening. It has been a day of great excitement here in the Old Market Square. It began much as the feast of Pentecost always begins here in the city, with lots of holiday-makers crowding the streets. There was nothing to suggest anything out of the ordinary. As far as I can discover, at about 8.30 this morning a group of the Jesus-followers came into the square from a nearby house where they had been staying. They were singing

117

and shouting out praises to God and were in a state of great excitement. A crowd collected round them to find out what was going on, and in next to no time an open-air public meeting had begun.

[*turns to 1st Bystander*]: Excuse me, sir. I believe you saw what happened here today.

1st B: Well, I don't know how it all started, I'm sure. But these Jesus-followers were all staying together in a house near the Square, and something happened there, I'm told. A noise like a powerful wind, some said it was. I didn't hear it myself. Mark you, they were talking and acting as though they were being swept along like a strong wind. *Something* had stirred them.

2nd B: I thought at first they were a bunch of cranks. All this enthusiasm. But the big fellow who did most of the talking was sane enough. He had the crowd spellbound.

R. Cohen [*turning towards the TV camera*]: The leader of the followers of Jesus is a Galilean fisherman called Simon Peter, and sometimes, the ' Big Fisherman ' because of his size. There is someone here who knows him.

[*turns to Miriam*]: What sort of person is this Peter? Do you know him well?

Miriam: I've seen him around the town a few times—with his mates—but never like this before.

R. Cohen: You mean he's different?

Miriam: I'll say he is. Crumbs, when I saw him a few weeks ago he was as frightened as a kitten; scared stiff. It was in the courtyard outside Herod's palace when his friend Jesus was being held for questioning. I knew they were mates and I told him so. D'you know, he swore they'd never met! I guess he must have been dead afraid that they'd take him ' inside ' too. [*Pause*]. But today he didn't show a shred of fear! He was talking about Jesus *openly* and there were scores of priests in the crowd ready to report back to the High Priest. I don't think he was worried any more about what might happen to him. He seems to have got something of his Master's spirit.

R. Cohen: [*turning to front*]: Yes, there were a number of priests and scribes in the crowd today, listening to Peter's speech. Let's talk to one of them now.

[*turns to Priest*]: Rabbi, what do *you* think of today's events?

Priest: I am afraid I have to take a very serious view of what has happened. Uneducated people of this sort have no right to take it upon themselves to teach others about God. This is a matter for the priests. As for the story about God raising Jesus from the dead; well this is plain nonsense. Blasphemy, in fact!

R. Cohen: On the other hand, Rabbi, their message seems to have won them 3,000 followers. Would this have happened if their story was based on a lie?

Priest: Oh, I think this is a flash in the pan. This new movement will die out in a few months—if the authorities allow it to last that long.

R. Cohen: [*turning to front*]: And now, finally, a word with the man who has been in the centre of things today—Simon Peter, a fisherman, a follower of Jesus and a man of obvious courage. Since he spoke to the large crowd here, he has been spending the last seven or eight hours talking to smaller groups and individuals. He must be a very tired man.
[*turning to Peter*]: Congratulation, Sir, you must feel very satisfied at the tremendous response to your speech.

Peter: What you have seen today is no credit to me. It is God's doing and to him we give the praise.

R. Cohen: Please don't misunderstand me, but I heard a number of people say that you and your friends were drunk when you came into the Square singing and shouting.

Peter: Drunk! At nine o'clock in the morning! Why, the pubs aren't even open at that time! No, what you saw and felt today was the very thing which our Master, Jesus, promised us before he left—the Holy Spirit. It is he who has given us the courage to speak—even when our knees were knocking.

R. Cohen: You now seem to have the beginning of a new movement. What are your next plans?

Peter: We have no plans. The Holy Spirit will show us what to do. In his strength we aim to carry on the Master's work.

R. Cohen: [*moving away from Peter*]: Today has been a day to remember. A day when a fisherman spoke to a vast crowd and God became real to many of them. The question we ask is 'Will the new movement last or will it fizzle out within this generation?'

This is Rachel Cohen, Israel TV, News at Nine.

THE KINGSHIP OF CHRIST

An Ascensiontide service first devised for Norwich Cathedral by Ida Shorter and Marjorie Parry, which could be adapted for use in smaller churches

It is not easy to provide something of a visual nature and to ensure that, without elaborate staging, it can be seen by over 1,000 children. This service, however, proved very popular and did not need a great deal of preparation. The theme was ' The Kingship of Christ ', chosen because the service was held on the Saturday after Ascension Day.

Information about music was given to the parishes beforehand, so that hymns and psalms could be practised, and there was a rehearsal of these in the Cathedral before the service began.

Duplicated work-books, based on the theme, were available for use afterwards.

For the children with speaking parts little rehearsal was necessary, but they met in the cathedral two or three times, mainly to accustom themselves to the use of the microphones.

When the procession entered, the Conductor went directly to the pulpit and after the banner bearers, clergy and choir (with whom the readers and soloist joined) had taken their places, the fanfare was sounded from the organ loft. Just as the congregation was expecting the service to begin, six children rushed up the aisle from the West End and, taking their places on a small platform near the lectern where microphones had been set up, they shouted, ' We heard the sound of trumpets. . . .' This certainly created an interest, which was maintained throughout the service.

If this service were held in a church, use could be made of mime or tableaux. Other hymns could be chosen, possibly with modern tunes. We should like to have sung ' Lift High the Cross ', while all the children followed the cross in procession at the close of the service, and this would be possible with a smaller number.

[*The congregation stand for the entrance of the choir and clergy. As they sit they hear a fanfare of (taped or recorded) trumpets. As this dies away, the children run up the aisle from the west door.*]

All children: We heard the sound of trumpets!

Child A: Yes, we heard the trumpets!

Child B: Is it a royal occasion?

Child C: Is there a king or queen here?

Conductor: It is a royal occasion, but no king or queen can be seen. The king we have come to praise is the king of kings: our Lord Jesus Christ. Let us praise him now by singing ' O Worship the King '.

Hymn: ' O Worship the King.'

Child A: Why do you call him king?

Conductor: He has always been thought of as king, even before he came on earth. Hear the teacher-prophets:

Reader 1: ' Behold, the days are coming,' says the Lord, ' when I will raise up for David a righteous branch, and he shall reign as king.'

Reader 2: Lo, your king comes to you; triumphant and victorious is he, humble and riding on an ass.

Child B: And when he was born, did they rejoice? Did they sound the trumpets?

Conductor: We read that apart from the shepherds, scarcely anyone noticed his birth, except for a few wise men.

All children: They saw a bright new star.

Conductor: They believed this bright new star to be a sign that a king was born.

Reader 1: Now when Jesus was born in Bethlehem of Judaea, in the days of Herod the king, behold, wise men from the East came to Jerusalem saying, ' Where is he who is born king of Jews? For we have seen his star in the east, and are come to worship him.'

Child 3: So the king who was born in a stable grew up as an ordinary boy?

Conductor: Not until he was a man did he start to make himself known. God used his cousin John to prepare people for him. Like the old teacher-prophets, John the Baptist saw him as king.

121

Reader 2: In those days came John the Baptist preaching in the wilderness of Judaea: ' Repent, for the kingdom of heaven is at hand.'

Conductor: So Jesus began his work: teaching, healing, loving. And the people of Israel thought: ' Here is our king at last.' He rode into Jerusalem on an ass, and they remembered their prophets had said: ' Lo, your king comes to you; triumphant and victorious is he, humble and riding on an ass.' And they sang praises to their king.

Hymn: ' All Glory, Laud and Honour.'

Conductor: But not all the people praised him. Some did not want him as king. So he was arrested and brought to Pilate. And this is what Pilate said: ' Art thou the king of the Jews ? ' Jesus answered: ' My kingdom is not of this world.' Pilate said unto him: ' Art thou a king, then ? ' Jesus answered: ' Thou sayest that I am a king. To this end have I been born and to this end am I come into the world.'

Child B: Even so they crucified him.

Conductor: Yes, he was crucified, dead and buried, but the third day he rose and for forty days he came and went among them. On one of those days he gave them this message: ' Full authority in heaven and on earth has been committed to me. Go forth, therefore, and make all nations my disciples; baptise men everywhere in the Name of the Father and of the Son and of the Holy Spirit, and teach them to observe all that I have commanded you. And be assured, I am with you always, to the end of time.' And soon after that he led them out as far as Bethany and blessed them with uplifted hands; and they returned to Jerusalem with great joy. Listen:

Solo [*sung*]: While they beheld, he was taken up and a cloud received him out of their sight. He ascended into heaven and sitteth on the right hand of God the Father.

Conductor: Now they knew what he meant when he said: ' My kingdom is not of this world.' So every year at this time his followers have remembered, and we remember now as we sing the glad Ascensiontide.

Hymn: ' Sing the Glad Ascensiontide.'

Prayers:

The Collect for Ascension Day.

Conductor: King of kings and lord of lords.
Thou art the king of glory, O Christ.
Thou art the everlasting Son of the Father.

Response: The Lord is king for ever and ever.

Conductor: Let us thank God
For sending Jesus to be our king.

Response: Thank you, God.

Conductor: For his life on earth.

Response: Thank you, God.

Conductor: For his suffering and death for us:

Response: Thank you, God.

Conductor: Because he reigns in heaven, yet is with us always.

Response: Thank you, God.

Conductor: Let us tell God we are sorry for the wrong things we have done.

All: Almighty God, our heavenly Father, have mercy upon us, Forgive us all our sins, Deliver us from all evil, Confirm and strengthen us in all goodness, And bring us to everlasting life, Through Jesus Christ our Lord. Amen.

Conductor: O Lord Jesus Christ, our king, help us always to be thy true and faithful followers.

All: Help us, O Lord.

Conductor: Help us always to be ready to serve thee, knowing that thou art with us always.

All: Help us, O Lord.
Teach us, good Lord,
To serve thee as thou deservest:
To give, and not to count the cost;
To fight, and not to heed the wounds;
To toil and not to seek for rest;
To labour and not to ask for any reward
Save that of knowing that we do thy will. Amen

All say The Lord's Prayer.

Hymn: ' We Have a King who Came to Earth.'

[*Collection and Offering*]

Bidding: All things come from thee, O God:

Response: And of thine own have we given thee.

[*All sing* Psalm 24.]

Blessing

Hymn: ' At the Name of Jesus.'

123

LET'S CELEBRATE ASCENSION DAY!

Alison Adcock describes an unrehearsed occasion of joy

We held an Ascension Day celebration in church for the fifty children, aged from 4 to 11, who come to our Saturday morning children's meeting. It was entirely unrehearsed, though the children knew all the songs except the homemade ' Our Marvellous King ', and you are therefore to imagine that the questions evoke answers from the children, that they volunteer for the various roles—and that anything can happen! I had a script to hand in case I lost the thread, but did not read my part, so it did not go word-for-word as written here.

Preparations and equipment

The sanctuary was decorated with vases of cow parsley and buttercups, and the frontal was white and gold.

We had made beforehand a demo-style banner of two sheets of white card, mounted back to back on laths. One side showed a ring of pink, brown, black and yellow boys and girls in bright frocks and jeans, dancing hand in hand round a crowned figure of Jesus, with the slogan, ' Jesus for King of Everywhere '. The other side read ' The Law of King Jesus: Love God most of all. Love each other all alike. Be friends.'

We also had made five nine-inch square cards, with letters on each side as follows: sh/p; a/e; l/a; o/c; m/e.

Our Easter Candle, which of course was still in church, has a dumpy candlestick and can stand on the altar. We made a crown of card covered in foil, beautifully spiky and large enough to fit over the holder and encircle the candle.

We made enough coloured paper crowns to give one to each child—for convenience of handling and so that the size was adjustable, these were made as strips of paper with two slide-on paperclips each.

We made two drums out of catering-size tins covered with crepe paper and with straps of twisted crepe paper to go round the drummer's neck. These were beaten with wooden spoons.

We also had to hand: a blue shawl; a gold lurex dress form a jumble sale, for an angel; a baby doll wrapped in cloth; a wooden box as a manger; three small blankets; a big bolster—or a Lilo or sleeping-bag would do; a laundry basket full of branches of greenery—we used box; a blindfold; a wooden platter on which were five bread rolls and two silver-paper fish; matches and taper; collecting bowl; hymn books all round; Bible; and a cushion.

I made a batch of bread rolls, one for everyone, spread them with butter and fish paste and put them on a large tray out of sight.

Songs and hymns used

' Shalom ' (*Faith, Folk and Clarity,* Galliard—but we ' Englished ' the words).

' Jesus bids us shine ', verse 1.

' Here we come with gladness ', verses 1 and 3 (*Hymns and Songs for Children,* SPCK).

' Let all the world in every corner sing ' (*Ancient and Modern Revised*).

' Go tell it on the mountains ', one verse (*FFC*).

' Jesus loves the little children '.

' Loving heavenly Father ' (*HSC*).

' The seven joys ', verses 1, 2, 3, 7 (*FFC*).

' Jesus shall reign ' (*AMR*).

' All glory, laud and honour ', 1 or 2 verses (*AMR*).

' Kumbaya ' (*FFC*).

' Lord of the Dance ' (*FFC*).

The ' Crown him ' verse from ' Praise him, praise him, all ye little children ' (*HSC*).

' Our marvellous King ' (home-made—to be found at the end of the article).

What happened

Today is Ascension Day. This is the day when, long ago, the friends of Jesus went up a mountain near Jerusalem. And as they stood on the top of the mountain they saw Jesus all shining bright and glorious, and then he left them and went to be with God for ever. Then they understood that he was more than just their friend—he was the King of the world, for ever and ever. Look, here's the banner that tells us—' Jesus, King of Everywhere '. [*Two children display banner*].

When a new king is crowned, we call the service a coronation, and today we are going to celebrate the coronation of King Jesus.

Here are the laws Jesus wants us all to keep [*turning the banner*]. Let's read them aloud.

Now, I need five people to help me ... here's one card each. On one side there's a red letter and on the other a green letter. Please will you hold up the card with the red letter in front. Do you know that word? Let's read it together:

sh–a–l–o–m

Say it again—shalom. It's not English, because Jesus didn't speak English, and this is a word that he often used when he met people. Jesus spoke the Jewish language. What does shalom mean in English? Would you turn the cards round, please, and show us? What's that word? Say it for me—' Peace '.

Jesus wished people ' Peace '—and peace means everyone happy and friendly together, no enemies, no fights. It's a good wish. Christians always wish each other peace at church on Sundays. The priest says to us, ' The peace of the Lord be always with you ' and we say, ' And with you '. Let's all say, ' The peace of the Lord to you ' ... and to show we mean it, let's shake hands, or hug each other like the footballers do. ...

Now we'll sing about it. Let's sing ' Shalom ' together:

' Shalom, dear friends, Shalom, dear friends, true peace and love,
Wherever we go God grant we may know true peace and love.'

The church is specially beautiful today. That's in honour of Jesus' coronation. Do you see the white and gold cloth on the altar? Do you see the flowers? What are the white ones called? The gold? Why do you think we chose white and gold? White stands for goodness and gold for a king, and Jesus is the best king that there ever could be.

Now I'm putting the big Easter candle in the middle of the altar. What does the candle mean? Who is it to remind us of? Jesus. So now we will put a crown over the Jesus candle. Here's a crown for Jesus. X [choose a child], will you take the crown on this cushion to the altar and put it over the candle, while we sing ' Crown him, crown him, all ye little children '?

When our King or Queen has been crowned here in England, all the Lords and Ladies put on their own crowns. We're going to have crowns just like them, to show that God thinks each one of us is a special and important person too! Let's all put on our crowns.

Now we'll light the great candle, and sing our candlelighting song. Who'll light the candle for us? [As this is done, sing ' Jesus bids us shine ', verse 1 only].

126

We have our gift of money for King Jesus, so let's make a procession to bring it to the altar. First the Jesus banner. Now, two drums ... and someone to carry the money. ... Now the drums can beat for us all to sing. [*All sing* ' Here we come with gladness ', verses 1 and 3. *After offertory, all return to their places, leaving money on altar and banner beside altar.*]

Now let us pray to God. Will you say the prayer after me? ' O God our Father, you know all about us. You know what makes us worried and miserable. You always understand, and you will always help us when we ask. Help us to think about your son, King Jesus. Help us to love him as he loves us. And help us to love each other. Amen.'

(If the children have individual prayers to offer, these could be used at this point.)

Now we'll sing a hymn, ' Let all the world in every corner sing '. What was the name of Jesus' mother? Who would like to come and be Mary for us? Here's a blue shawl to wrap over your head and all round you. [*Choose and dress the angel, remind the children of the Annunciation story, and let them act it or mime it to a reading. Talk about the Nativity:* ' What did Mary use for a cot? What's a manger usually used for? ...' *and establish the shepherds at a distance, minding their sheep, while Mary places the baby in the manger. Act or mime the angel's message and the journey to Bethlehem.*] The shepherds came and looked for Jesus and Mary, and they knelt down and worshipped their King. Let's sing about it—let's sing, ' Go tell it on the mountains '.

Was Mary happy when Jesus was born? Yes, of course. It was her First Good Joy. So we'll sing about that, too: ' The first good joy that Mary had ', verse 1 and chorus.

When Jesus grew up he helped lots of people, and that made Mary very happy, too. Do you remember the story of the lame man who lay on a mattress and had to be carried everywhere? [*Children can talk about and act or mime the story. Equip the lame man with a bolster or lilo to discard.*] I'll bet the lame man was so happy that he skipped and danced because he could move his legs again! You do that while we sing, ' The second good joy. ...'

Now, will someone come and be the poor blind beggar called Bartimaeus? I'll bandage your poor sore eyes. Now you can't see anything. ... What do you most want Jesus to do for you? ... And so he did! [*Whisk away the blindfold.*] Let's sing ' The next good joy. ...'

How many joys did Jesus give Mary altogether? Let's sing about the seventh one. Do you remember—it was when she saw him wearing the crown of heaven. ...

Jesus is the King of Everywhere. Another hymn tells us about that. Let's sing ' Jesus shall reign. . . .'

Now I want you to listen to Y, who will read to us from the Bible about Jesus and some children that he met one day. In the days when Jesus lived, long ago, grown-up people hadn't much time for children. They pushed them out of the way and told them not to be a nuisance. Some people are still a bit like that, aren't they? But Jesus wasn't. Listen. (Mark 10. 13–16 *is read in a modern version*.)

Shall we sing about Jesus and children? ' Jesus loves the little children.' Let's kneel down and pray to God for children everwhere. [*Sing, kneeling, ' Loving heavenly Father '*.]

Do you remember the day that Jesus rode into Jerusalem? Tell me about it . . . what did the children do? . . . what did they shout? Hosanna is a prayer as well as a cheer—a bit like God Save the King. I think we should make a procession like that for Jesus now. Look, I've got branches for you to wave. Come and get your branches and we'll march round the church waving them, and we'll shout Hosanna! Hosanna! [*During procession, sing ' All glory, laud and honour '*, *two verses*.] Now we'll put the branches away. . . .

Let's kneel down quietly and say a prayer to Jesus. I'll say one line and then you say, ' Help us to help you ':

Lord Jesus Christ, you are our King:
R. Help us to help you.
You love all children:
You want us to love each other:
You want us all to be friends:
You want us to help each other:
R. Help us to help you. Amen

[*short silence*]

One day Jesus went for a long walk with a big crowd of thousands of people. They walked for miles along the shore of a lake and up the grassy slopes of a hill. Let's pretend to be that crowd. Come for a walk with me! (The walk can be out into the churchyard or into a chapel or the chancel, according to circumstances.) Now we're climbing the hill . . . it's hot and we're all tired. Let's sit down and rest. It's been a long walk and we're all feeling hungry. What can we have to eat? Has anyone got any food? Jesus hasn't. Nor have any of his friends. But there's a little boy whose Mum has given him a picnic. Z, did you know your Mum had given you a picnic? Well, you look over there! [*The platter with the fish and rolls is found and and produced.*] The boy wants to share his picnic with Jesus, and Jesus wants to share it with everyone. And so he does, because there's enough for everybody! [*Produce tray and eat rolls together.*]

Now I want you to help me sing a song about King Jesus. It goes to the tune of ' Glory, glory, alleluia ', but the chorus ends up a bit differently. [*Sing together chorus, then organise who sings verses—perhaps older children, who can read easily? or teachers only? All join in chorus. Words of ' Our Marvellous King ' will be found at end of article.*]

Well, if Jesus is our King, we must keep his laws. Do you remember them? Let's have another look. [*Produce banner again.*] Love God most, love each other all alike. And loving means helping and being friends. It isn't easy to keep these laws. We shall need Jesus' help. So let's kneel down and quietly ask Jesus to come and help us, using the African song ' Kumbaya, my Lord ', which means ' Come by here, come to this place '. [*Sing ' Kumbaya ', kneeling.*]

Jesus taught us how to pray to God. So, as our saviour Christ has commanded and taught us, we are bold to say: [*Say together*] ' Our Father. . . .'

Now let's sing and dance all round the church for Jesus. The song is ' Lord of the Dance '!

Three cheers for King Jesus! . . .

And now [*quietly*] ' May the grace . . . Amen.'

Our Marvellous King

(To the tune of ' John Brown's Body ', slightly adapted. The last line of the chorus is as follows):

Oh what a marvel-lous king, Je - sus, Oh what a marvel - lous king

When móst kings léad their ármies óut it's péople thát they sláy,
But Jésus léads his Chrístíans to dríve all páin awáy,
When sómebody's made háppy then we knów he's wón the dáy,
Oh whát a márvellous kíng.

 Glory, glory alleluia; Glory, glory alleluia; Glory, glory alleluia;
 Oh what a marvellous King, Jesus, Oh what a marvellous king.

Now most kings give the millionaires a banquet and a ball;
The poor folk stand outside and sigh and wait for crumbs to fall;
But Jesus gives a picnic and there's plenty for us all,
Oh what a marvellous king.

No king on earth can heal the sick or make the lame to run;
But Jesus made the dumb folk sing and blind men see the sun;
And Christians all obey him when they're helping everyone;
Oh what a marvellous king.

I   129

Now most kings go a-riding in a car that's bullet-proof;
But Jesus rode a donkey with a clippy-cloppy hoof;
The children ran beside him and their cheering raised the roof,
Oh what a marvellous king.

Now most kings rule a single land or two or three or four,
They rule them for a dozen years or else perhaps a score;
But Jesus rules the whole wide world, he's king for evermore,
Oh what a marvellous king.

GOOD ST SWITHUN

is remembered by Hilda Rostron

St Swithun's Day, if thou dost rain,
for forty days it will remain:
St Swithun's Day, if thou be fair,
for forty days t'will rain no mair.

This verse, which is very old, is a rhyme which many mothers and grandmothers remember. Swithun is said to have been a humble, kind man who lived from about the year 800 to 862. This was during the reigns of the Saxon kings Egbert and Ethelwulf.

Winchester was at this time a most important city and Swithun was made the Bishop of the diocese by Ethelwulf. He had been tutor to Ethelwulf when he was a young prince.

Swithun did a great deal of good for the churches in his diocese and the city as a whole. He left instructions that when he died he should be buried on a path outside the church where people passed by. After about a hundred years it was decided that his bones be placed within the cathedral in a shrine. This was done with great pomp and ceremony. It seems strange that this good and gentle man should be remembered in the main for the ' rain rhyme ', but probably the country people believed that humble Bishop Swithun did not want his bones to be moved from the outside pathway. During the translation, the monks who were removing the body had to stop work for the persistent rain that fell. Whatever the origin of the legend, the rhyme is still to this day believed. Few people, however, actually bother to count the wet days following a wet St Swithun's!

Fruit farmers, however, say that rain on the fifteenth of July is especially good for apples. They call it ' St Swithun christening the little apples '. Whatever we think, we do well to remember that Swithun was not just a figure in a legend, but a good and well-loved bishop, friend and counsellor—and it is hardly fair to blame him if the rain spoils our holiday! Let us be thankful, instead, for the life of one of God's hard-working saints.

A PROJECT FOR HARVEST

Joyce Gray describes a three-week course of lessons which add concern for others to the theme of thanksgiving

One way in which we can make the Harvest Thanksgiving service of practical value is to use it as a children's offering service in which, as a thanksgiving for God's gifts to them, the children give money as a positive way of helping other children less fortunate than they. The aim of our project is to try to inspire in the children a feeling of thankfulness for their own good fortune.

The three weeks' preparation will include three things:

(1) Arousing interest and consequent learning concerning the sorts and conditions of needy children in the world today.

(2) Creating meaningful prayers in the children's own mode of expression, some of which will be used during the service.

(3) Learning the tunes and words of the hymns to be used in the service.

Week I

The group leaders should introduce the theme at the children's own level of experience, along the following lines:

' Saying "thank you"': do you remember being taught to use these two little words? They are words which can make such a difference. Our days are filled with the gifts which God gives us. If, at the end of each day we counted up God's blessings to us, we would be very surprised. Let us make a list of the ordinary things which happen in a day, which we take so much for granted. Remember that everything is a gift from God, however small.'

A list of examples for group leaders:

water which helps us to wake up in the morning
breakfast
clothes
television
school, teachers and friends
postmen
the street, passers-by, cars, etc.

Each group can devise their own way of compiling the list, but a satisfactory method is for each group to have a large sheet of paper and a felt pen, and for someone to write each item as a child suggests it.

Another method would be for individual children in the group to tear from a piece of newspaper the shape of one thing for which they are thankful, and for the rest of the group to guess what it is—or for each child in turn to draw a shape on a central piece of paper for the others to guess.

The group leader will need to draw the lesson to a close by reading the list, or listing the objects drawn or torn out, and perhaps saying, ' Yes we have a great deal to say " thank you " for. God is very good to us.'

One such actual list read as follows:

> water
> soap
> food
> clothing
> comics
> school
> friends
> teachers
> parents
> brothers and sisters
> telly
> fires
> books
> smiles

The children should be encouraged to write ' thank you ' prayers at home and to bring them the next week.

Examples of ' thank you ' prayers made up by the children:

> Thank you for our clothing,
> and the water we drink.
> Thank you for the flowers
> that make the world lovely.
> Thank you for the trees.
>
> *Karen Hunter*

Thank you, Father, for the wheat,
Thank you for the food we eat.
Thank you for the apples red,
Thank you for our cosy bed.
Thank you for the birds that fly,
Thank you for the bright blue sky.
Thank you for the eggs that the hen laid,
Thank you, God, for all you've made.

Moira Livingstone

Thank you for flowers that brighten our day,
Flowers that are bright and gay,
Thanks for the school we attend each day,
We thank you, Lord, in every way.

Julie Tate

Thank you for the bread,
You give us too much
Give the others more.
Help to grow food for others to buy
And to send away.
Help us not to be unkind.
Thank you for lots of other things. Amen.

Diane Davison

Thank you God for everything,
The running water that we see,
The apples in the apple tree.
The birds that sing sweetly overhead
The garden and the garden shed.
Thank you for the clothes we wear,
The pretty ribbons in our hair.
Thank you, God, for us and other people
        in far off countries.
Thank you, God, for everything.
Thank you, God.

Gillian Cooper

Thank you God for the world and the
trees and the flowers and our houses
and our clothes and for our mothers
and fathers and brothers and sisters
and babies. God, I thank you for our
love for you. God, I know you love us
very, very well. I praise you, God,
almighty.

                    Amen.

Week II

When we did this course, we began the second week by making a ' Thank you, God ' chart. This was done together, before we broke up into groups. As each child offered his thought, it was entered into the appropriate column, with his name alongside.

	Gift	Name
	Sun	Robert
	Food	Deborah
	Clothes	Kay
	Sweets	Susan
I thank	School	Kevin
God for:	Water	Pamela
	Sunday school	Lynn
	Parents	Jacqueline
	Brothers	Alan
	Our life	Tom
	Church	Valerie
	Flowers	Paul

After compiling this, we used two of the prayers which were made up by the children, so that the intercessions were really meaningful. The prayers were mounted on to card, again to give the children a sense of satisfaction in knowing that their efforts are appreciated. If their efforts are ignored and never seen again, it is not surprising if the children are not found to be very co-operative next time anything is asked of them.

When we divided into groups for the second part of the theme, in our case the recapping of the previous week's thinking had been done. Otherwise the group leaders' first task would have been quickly to recap on the previous week's discoveries. The children were then reminded how lucky they are to be able to enjoy all these things. Then they were asked to think about other boys and girls who are not so lucky at the present time: boys and girls just like them, suffering the effects of a devastating and terrible war. How would the children feel? They would be frightened, and we knew that they were starving. The group leader can elaborate as follows:

' Because they are hungry, they have no energy or life. They sit staring into space for hour after hour. Some die as they sit, others are packed into over-crowded hospitals and again many die. Many boys and girls will never grow up into men and women, as you will.'

We talked about other children who were suffering in various parts of the world, drawing on newspapers and TV news for our information. Again they were asked to make up prayers about these situations.

Week III

Again we began with another look at the ' Thank you, God ' chart, and this time, in our opening worship, we used one of the prayers for children in need.

This week, in the groups, the children were asked to think about children in our own land who are not privileged as they are.

The groups listed:

(a) crippled children who can never run and play;

(b) blind children who will never see the colours of flowers nor see ordinary things;

(c) deaf children who will never hear and never talk properly;

(d) deaf, dumb and blind children, who will only know that people touch their hands, and who will only ever contact the world by touch. They live in a world of darkness and silence;

(e) children who will never be able to think and work and talk as we can;

(f) spastic children who cannot move their legs and arms as we can, and who cannot control their movements;

(g) children who have had to be taken from their homes and be looked after by other people;

(h) children whose parents do not want them;

(i) children who have no nice things to wear, who never have new clothes, whose clothes are bought at jumble sales. Their new clothes are those which boys and girls like us have finished with.

It is important that the list discussed is used with discretion, and that the children's home backgrounds are known to the group leaders. For instance, our group leaders were equipped with a list at their preparation class, so that they were prepared if the children did not come forward with suggestions. They were warned not to talk about category (g) in one of our departments where we do have children from a local authority group home, or category (e) in the department where we have two educationally sub-normal children. In some areas, obviously, the last category would not be mentioned, but in an area where the children are well cared for, it is good that they should be aware of other children who are not so fortunate.

Finally, the children were brought together and told about the children's offering service to be held the following Sunday. It was to be in the afternoon, and parents and children were given an invitation. They were told that at Harvest this year we would show our thanks to God by giving money to help people suffering in other parts of the world. Each child was given an envelope, and asked to give some of his pocket money and to see if parents and relatives would help. We had a most successful service and, I think, succeeded in our aim of arousing the children's interest in and compassion for the less fortunate, as well as sincerely saying ' thank you ' to God for our everyday blessings.

HUNGRY AT HARVEST

Joyce G. Gray describes the service which formed the culmination of her three-week course

Each department of our Sunday school had a banner made for the occasion, with three bearers—one carrying the departments' offering envelopes in a polythene bag. Two other banners led the procession; the first was that which we take to the diocesan Sunday School Festival each year, bearing the name of our church, ' Holy Spirit, Denton '. The second bore the slogan, ' We have, they need '. All in all, therefore, the procession would consist of six banners and fourteen children. We rehearsed, very carefully, in the church on the Sunday afternoon. (The children feel more confident if this is done, and it is important that the procession is done well, as it is to the glory of God.)

Two other young people were approached and bravely agreed to take part in the service. The boy was twelve years old, and the girl fourteen. Ann is now acting as a Sunday school Assistant in one of the kindergarten departments, until she is old enough actually to teach. They were to speak a dialogue in place of the address. We felt that it would be much more realistic if the children took as much part as possible, and probably the children and people would listen more attentively, if they saw young people in the front, instead of the Vicar. Again rehearsals took place until we were sure that Ann and Tom felt confident, and that their voices were carrying throughout the large church, right to the back of the balcony.

The actual service was held in the afternoon of our Harvest Thanksgiving day. The church was only decorated with flowers, as the whole congregation had been asked to make a money gift to be given to Inter-Church Aid. The church looked lovely, but two placards placed on the front of the lectern and pulpit, showing starving Africans, were a stark miserable sight in the midst of such beauty. These placards helped to bring home the frank truth that we have much, in contrast to many people in the world.

The attendance surpassed all our hope—the church was full to overflowing. There were families of Sunday school children, young people from the organisations and adult members of the church. It was a very fine family occasion. The service was simple, and some of the children's own prayers were used for the intercessions. Usually during the address there is an air of restlessness on such an occasion, but not this time. We need not have feared for the courage of Ann and Tom; they spoke out clearly and with conviction, and their message came through.

Ann: Hello, Tom—haven't seen you for ages. How's things?

Tom: All right. You look loaded.

Ann: I am! Oh dear, it's a long way from Chapel House with all this stuff.

Tom: Yes, you'd better put them down for a minute or two, and listen to this. It's worth hearing.

Lesson: The story of the Good Samaritan from the *New English Bible*.

Ann: Whatever did you want to listen to that for? I've heard it dozens of times—at school, in church, in Sunday school. You get a bit sick of the same old story. I know I've got to help my neighbour.

Tom: Don't be so sure that you do. I thought that too, but you know, it's easy to talk, don't you think?

Ann: What do you mean? I do know. My neighbour means everyone I meet. What else is there to know?

Tom: Well—I've been thinking recently—I've just had a good dinner today. Have you?

Ann: Oh yes—marvellous. Roast lamb, roast potatoes, peas, mint sauce, ordinary potatoes, then jelly, fruit and cream. I look forward to Sunday dinner.

Tom: Yes, but did you realise that lads and girls just like us have a pain inside all day long, that their stomachs are all swollen up, and that their legs and arms are like matchsticks? They just sit staring because they haven't got the strength to walk— doctors say they will never live. We will grow up and enjoy living: many of them will die very soon.

Ann: Oh don't be so morbid! I know! It's terrible, but we can't help it.

Tom: No. I know we can't, but maybe we could *do* something for them. You're just talking like the man who passed by on the other side, if you take that attitude. Millions of people in the world are hungry today; we've had plenty, and we just don't care. That can't be right.

139

Ann: It can't be as bad as all that!

Tom: Oh, but it is. One-third of all the people in the world are starving. You'll probably live and get your old age pension, but heaps of people in India only live until they are 26, because they aren't properly fed. I saw a film where the children were eating dirt off the ground because they were so hungry. It doesn't seem right to have a Sunday dinner like mine, and for them to have nothing.

Ann: I'm beginning to see what you mean about passing by on the other side. These people need us to help.

Tom: I've heard it said that we'll never be through trying to feed our hungry brothers and sisters in other lands, but I'm sure our Lord wants us to keep trying to help.

Ann: Well, there are easier things to do—I mean, I help the old lady across the road, and I say my prayers—and—

Tom: It doesn't alter the fact that you've had too much to eat today, like me, and our brothers and sisters are hungry. Our dogs feed better than they do.

Ann: Well, I've brought my tin of peas, and some sugar and some tea. I don't suppose it's much help. Anyway, where's yours? You can talk—looks as if you haven't brought anything, after all you've had to say!

Tom: No, I haven't. It's different this year. In our church we aren't going to pass by on the other side. I don't know where you've been! Didn't you hear that instead of tins and packets of food, we were all going to collect money in an envelope, and bring that as our offering today [*holds up envelope*]? All the money we bring will be sent to the people who are in need of food or medical care, wherever there is disaster. We are like the Samaritan then—we're really trying to help! But really we should keep on helping, so I've made this money box [*holds it up*] and I'm going to put some of my pocket money in every week, and then send it away when the box is full. This envelope today is only a beginning.

Ann: I'm with you now! I see what God wants of us this harvest. We can go on enjoying our good meals, if we are trying to help those in need as well. Jesus said in that story, ' Go and act now! '

As the dialogue ended, the vicar came forward and asked the children in the congregation to stand. Then he said, ' These people whom you have heard about need help. Who will help them?' The children responded loudly, 'We will', and then the offertory hymn began. Down the centre aisle came the dignified procession of banners. In turn the offerings were presented, and then the banners processed up the centre aisle until they were evenly spaced from the back in the front of the church. Then they turned to face the altar, as the vicar presented their offerings and pronounced the blessing. This impressive and moving service was geared to the needs of the children, and was a service with enough dignity and meaning to impress the many adults there.

NEIGHBOURS
by Ivy Russell
A harvest-time story

' Aha, the house next door has been sold at last! ' said Mr Robinson.
' Perhaps our new neighbours will tidy up that dreadful mess in
the garden! '

You couldn't blame Mr Robinson for grumbling. He had just
retired from work, and he spent most of his time keeping his own
garden neat and tidy. But on the other side of the fence the grass
and weeds were waist high, and every day a few more dandelion
seeds came floating across into his rose-bed. So when a removal
van drew up next door, and then a battered old car stopped right
behind it, Mr Robinson was soon at the window, peeping through
the curtains for a glimpse of his new neighbours. But he wasn't
at all pleased when he saw a lady with a baby in her arms, followed
by four small children and their father!

The removal men carried the furniture in, while the children dashed
all around, looking for their favourite toys and storing them safely
away in odd corners. Next day their father put up a clothes-line
and their mother hung out lots and lots of washing.

But nobody had time for any gardening!

Mr Robinson was so miserable that he stayed indoors for a
whole month, wishing that the new neighbours would go away
again. But one day when he was looking out of the window a
ball came sailing over the fence. Mr Robinson was so cross
that he marched straight out into the garden, where two of the
boys were peeping over the fence. ' Please, mister,' one of them
began. Mr Robinson threw the ball back, but the boys didn't
move. ' Well, what do you want? ' he said grumpily. ' Please,
mister, why don't you pick your apples? They're lovely and ripe! '
Startled, Mr Robinson looked up at the tree, which had grown far
too big for him to manage any more. The other boy said, ' If you
can't reach them, we could do it for you. We'd like to, honestly! '
' You're far too small to get up that tree,' growled Mr Robinson.
' Besides, your mother wouldn't allow it.' ' Oh, I don't mind! '
said a cheery voice from among the washing. ' I like to see my
boys making themselves useful. That's what neighbours are
for, isn't it? '

So the boys came into the garden and swarmed up the tree, and
spent a happy afternoon picking apples and collecting them
carefully in a bag slung around their necks. Afterwards Mr Robinson gave them a basketful to take back home. ' So that's what
neighbours are for! ' he said to himself. ' Well, a few dandelions
aren't so very important. I wonder if their mother would let them
come to the Zoo next Saturday? '

WHO ARE THE STARVED?

A meditation for Harvest by Pamela Egan

A hot, dusty market-place in southern France.
Too hot to do more than gossip in the shade.
But on the dry gravel stands a woman selling
   balloons
And a boy.
He needs decent shoes.
He needs a coat better than this hand-down from
   his brothers.
He needs nourishing food.
But he wants a balloon.
He stands in the dust and wants a lovely, useless,
   unattainable bubble
Glittering on the end of a string.

At this time of harvest
We thank God for his mercies to us
And we pray for those in desperate need.
Let us also remember
Those who are not starving, but starved:
Children with a roof over their heads in a fine new flat
But nowhere to play;
Children with a television set
But no-one who will ever switch it off;
Children who are afraid of silence
And need the reassurance of the transistor;
Children whose reaction to an insect is, ' What's
   that ? I don't know—kill it ';
Children who have everything they need
And do not know what is worth wanting.

At this time of harvest
Let us ask God for grace
To tend these thin, starved lives
That they may grow into triumphant fullness.
Let us ask it for the sake of his Son,
Who knows the true value of a couple of sparrows—
Or a one-franc balloon.

143

THE GIFT OF RAIN

Alan Beck offers an alternative to the traditional Harvest theme

Harvest Festival—it is always a puzzle to find some new angle! Why not start with a riddle?

' You cannot see it, for it has neither shape nor colour, you cannot taste or smell it, but it is quite heavy. When astronauts went to the Moon they did not find any of it there—so they could only bring back dust and stones; no plants, no living creature of any kind. For these all must have . . . *water.*'

That was how we began our Family Service in our little village. And from somewhere with no water at all, we went on to think about a country which has only two lots of rain each year (Palestine) and where these rains sometimes fail. We read about the time when the rains failed for three years running, of Elijah's prayer, and of the downpour that followed (1 Kings 18). Then we acted out the story. The children left the pews to stand in any convenient open space. The adults remained in their seats to be the sound effects department.

First the children looked at the dry, dusty ground, let it trickle through their fingers, scribbled in it or threw it into the air. They felt the pain of hunger and, especially, thirst. They swooned to the ground in the heat. Then a rumour spread: ' The prophet says that we are to eat and drink!' Now they knelt to pray with Elijah. They strained their eyes towards the west, but shook their heads as they could see nothing. Disappointed, they prayed again . . . and looked again. Six times they prayed, six times they looked growing more and more disheartened. The seventh time they prayed almost in despair.

But now, when they looked, one or two saw a tiny cloud. They pointed it out to the others. Now all pointed and followed the progress of the clouds as they moved across the sky. Now the whole sky was black. They stretched out their hands to feel the first drops of rain. Now they began to hear it, softly at first, ' pitter, patter '. The children sniffed the moist air, cupped their hands and rubbed their faces and arms with the soft rainwater. Now the noise of rain increased ' splish-splash ' and the children began to dance for joy. Now the adults clapped and stamped their feet as we

144

imagined the thunder crashing and rain pelting down. The children splashed their feet in imaginary puddles in a climax of excitement.

At a signal the thunder died away and the children saw that streams were now gushing down the hillside. Eagerly they knelt and sucked up long noisy drinks. They were much too thirsty to worry about manners, or mud in the water! Then, to bring the mime to an end, all stood and shouted ' Hallelujah! '

After a rehearsal and a couple of performances it was time to move on to somewhere that we often think has too much rain: ' Rain, rain, go to Spain, never show your face again.' We listened to a typical English weather forecast, read by a newsreader holding up an open umbrella. We saw how we take this gift too much for granted, just as we sometimes take God's love for granted; there is more of this also than we deserve. So we came to Matthew 5: ' He sends his rain on honest and dishonest alike '. Now we were ready to offer our harvest gifts—and pride of place was given to a large glass jug of water.

THE VINEYARD

A story for harvest time
by Dory Fisher

There was once a farmer, who lived with his twin sons Karl and Hans in a beautiful valley in Germany. Each side of the grey stone farmhouse in which they lived, the ground sloped gently upwards, catching every ray of sunshine. It was filled with row upon row of neat grapevines which the farmer looked after carefully from year to year. Now the farmer, a simple man, brought his sons up in the only way he knew how, and that was to work on the land. He never bothered to send them to school. The two boys spent their time learning how to loosen the rich soil ready for the plants, to strengthen the stakes that would hold the growing vines, and to watch out for spring frosts, grass and weeds, that could so easily ruin the crop of juicy blue-black grapes that were gathered each autumn.

As the boys grew stronger and taller, and the farmer older and more feeble, he sent Karl off to care for the ground that sloped to the right-hand of the farmhouse, and Hans to care for the ground that sloped to the left. He himself spent more time around the house, doing the smaller tasks that had to be done. But he spent long afternoons in his rocking chair on the verandah, gazing worriedly out at his two sons as they toiled on the slopes. For the farmer had a problem. 'Which son shall I leave in charge of the vineyards when I die?' he wondered. 'Shall it be Karl, who is so quick, and finishes his work in half the time that it takes his brother? Or shall it be Hans? For although Hans is much slower, he rarely breaks the young shoots, or bruises the ripe fruit with impatient hands, as Karl does.'

To the old man it was really a puzzle, for the land meant a great deal to him. So day after day he brooded, until one spring afternoon he suddenly had an idea.

After the three had their supper that evening, he said to Karl and Hans, 'Tomorrow I am going away, and I shall not come back until the grapes are ready for picking. The one whose slope yields the most fruit, is the one that I will leave in charge of all the vineyards when I die.'

After his father had left the next morning, Karl laughed mockingly at Hans.

146

'You'll see,' he boasted, 'I shall be in charge of the vineyards. You are too slow even to catch a snail.' Hans didn't answer, he felt too sad at not seeing the familiar figure of his father sitting beside the hearth.

Now there was no holding Karl back. Each day he was up at the crack of dawn. Striding swiftly to his slope, he was soon at work with his fast, nimble hands. Being very greedy, he had made up his mind that not only was he going to be in charge of both the vineyards, he wanted them both to belong to him. All the time he worked, he fretted and complained.

'There's not enough rain,' he grumbled. 'There's no warmth in the sun.' Nothing was right. He was forever scheming and planning other ways to make his slope the best.

Hans, however, just kept steadily and slowly on in his old way. Patiently he would coax a growing plant around a stake, or would bend down to look long and carefully at the young roots, to make sure that no grass or weeds were choking them. He neither cared nor worried about being in charge of the vineyards. He felt only the contentment of the sun warm on his back, and he loved the land as his father did.

One day Karl, looked up into the clear blue sky and thought, 'If only I had the sun all to myself, and it shone only on MY side, then without a doubt, I should have the best crop of fruit.'

No sooner had the idea struck him than he decided that it would be quite a simple matter to arrange. You remember that he had not had any schooling, and knew very little about the ways of the world?

'All I have to do,' he said to himself, 'is wait until the sun falls down behind the hills, then go and fetch it back here. I won't be away for long, and everything here will still carry on growing while I'm gone.'

To him, it seemed a wonderful idea. The next morning, without saying a word to Hans, he set out.

When Hans saw Karl leave the valley, he thought it very odd, but as the vines on his slope were now growing thicker and taller, there was so much extra work to do that he soon forgot about his brother's strange behaviour.

When the hot summer weather brought the thunder rumbling, and the lightning flashing across the valley, and heavy rain from low dark clouds beat down the stakes, Hans was soon busy repairing those on his side of the farmhouse. Those on Karl's side lay flattened where the water had broken them.

While Karl still journeyed on over mountains and through dense forests in search of the sun (which somehow never seemed to get any nearer) pests and plant diseases attacked the growing buds.

147

Hans quickly sprayed the plants to save the coming blossom, but many of those over on the right-hand slope just withered away and died.

As the buds opened up into flowers, then shed their tiny petals to leave small berries that would later on ripen into large honey-sweet grapes, huge flocks of greedy birds swooped down to peck them. But Hans had worked hard to make bird-scarers to frighten them away. Squawking angrily, they rose with a flutter of wings to Karl's slope where they soon pecked clean any fruit that had survived the bad weather.

As summer turned into autumn, Hans was walking along his terraced slope one day, gently feeling the full grapes to make sure that they were not over-ripe, when he looked up and saw his father walking towards him. Joyfully he showed him the dark green vines, heavy with bunches of luscious blue-black grapes.

Then the old farmer raised his head and looked across at the other side of the valley. He saw the answer to his problem in the desolate ground, broken stakes and yellow, fruitless vines.

Far away in that fertile valley Hans, who was content to work hard for what he got, now owns both slopes, and is rich enough to hire other hands to help him—while Karl, his clothes tattered and torn, is still somewhere out in the wide, wide world, still thinking that everything will come right if he can only grab for himself something that can never be his.

LAST-MINUTE THINGS TO MAKE FOR HARVEST

Some useful ideas from Hilda Rostron

Make together a Harvest frieze with flowers, fruit and vegetables cut from magazines to fasten to a screen or wall. Make golden-coloured streamers with crepe paper and with Sellotape fasten these to a variety of *real* fruit, etc. arranged upon a harvest table where all can appreciate the theme.

Plan a 'reflection on harvest' with the aid of a large mirror and a flower and autumn leaf layout, to achieve twice the value in brightness.

An easy-to-do poster is an eye-catcher for anywhere in school or in church. Cut out deep gold sheaf or bale shapes and *lightly* gum them on to a 'field' background of pale yellow. A three-dimensional effect can be made if the sheaf shape is bent forward from the background, or if bales can be made from cubes of gold paper. A strip of blue paper is the horizon and dabs of fluffed cottonwool form clouds.

Teachers could fill empty mustard-and-cress punnets with fruit, nuts and sweets (sugar harvest), plus an autumn leaf or a few flower-heads as gifts to give as 'Thank God for harvest' presents for the younger children.

WHEN FIELDS ARE GOLDEN

Moderato

Words and Music by Noel Connell
Arr: Eddie Pearl

When fields are gol-den and or—chards are done,———, And

back to the har-bours the li—ttle ships come,———

It seems so li—ttle, for so much to say,———

Words that mean "Thank You, dear God," when we pray.

Rall ····· Last verse ·····

150

WHEN FIELDS ARE GOLDEN
A hymn by Noel Connell

1. When fields are golden and orchards are done,
       And back to the harbours the little ships come,
    It seems so little, for so much, to say
       Words that mean ' Thank you, dear God,' when we pray.

2. Thanks for the farmers, their combines and ploughs,
       Tractors in furrows and blossoms on boughs,
    Apples in season, as calendars spin,
       Working and watching and gathering in.

3. Care for the fishermen, out on the deep,
       Bringing their harvest while young children sleep,
    Food for the table, a quicksilver store,
       Trawling and hauling and heading for shore.

IAN'S HARVEST

A seasonal story for the younger ones, by Ivy Russell

It all started last springtime, when Ian's father was digging over the garden ready to plant his vegetables. Ian stood watching, and suddenly he remembered the rosy apples and the fine carrots and marrows that he had seen the year before, at the harvest festival. How everbody had admired them! Ian thought how exciting it would be to have everybody praising the things you had grown, and he said, ' Daddy, I want to grow a marrow of my very own. Will you show me what to do?'

So daddy gave him a corner of the garden, and a packet of seeds, and showed him what to do. Ian planted his seeds, and then every day he went out to see if anything was happening.

At last the little green shoots appeared, and the marrow plants began to creep along the ground. Then came the yellow flowers and finally—the very first marrow appeared! It grew . . . and it grew . . . and it grew.

By October it was absolutely ENORMOUS, and Ian was dizzy with happiness. When the harvest festival came his father lifted it into the small wheelbarrow, and Ian pushed it round to the church. All the way he was practising the prayer he would say:

' Look at the marrow I've brought for you, Father God! Aren't I clever to grow one as big as this!'

Ian had almost reached the church when a little girl came out of her gate, carrying an egg very carefully in her hands. Crash! The wheelbarrow bumped into her, and the egg fell on the pavement and smashed.

' Oh, look what you've done!' said Susan, and tears began to roll down her cheeks.

' Pooh! It's only an egg!' said Ian. 'You can buy dozens like that at the shop. Look at my marrow! I grew this myself.'

' It was the first egg my little hen Whitey had ever laid,' said Susan. 'You only put your seeds in the ground, and God did all the real work. '

Suddenly Ian felt quite ashamed, because what she said was true.

' I'll tell you what,' he said. ' We'll both take the marrow, and it can be a present from both of us.' So he took one handle of the barrow and Susan took the other, and they pushed it into church together.

He thought of a new prayer, too. ' Please, God, help Whitey to lay another egg tomorrow.'

And Whitey did, so everybody was happy.

ST LUKE: WRITER PHYSICIAN ARTIST

A project for juniors by Helen Fullmer, which could be worked through as preparation for a St Luke's-tide service or as a holiday course

Aim   To help children to appreciate the importance of St Luke's gifts and skills.

1.   LUKE THE WRITER

   (*a*)   Look at and discuss school or class library. Write down titles of three favourite books (perhaps one only for younger children) and say who wrote, illustrated and published them, what they are about and why they are ' favourite '.

   (*b*)   Re-visit library and note how books are classified. List some of the classifications, e.g. books for entertainment (fiction and adventure) books for information (science, history, geography etc.), books on arts (music, poetry, painting) books of instruction (cookery, handicrafts, first aid), books about people (biographies, the Bible). Writers of books are usually people who are experts in their own field (find examples) or who have something special to say, e.g. writers of the Bible. List names of known writers and what sort of book they write. The Bible is a library of all sorts of books. Look at the New Testament and note names of writers, particularly of Gospels.

   Was St Luke a historian? Biographer?

   Make a book and if possible *write* its contents (or for younger children, choose a subject and illustrate it fully in strip-cartoon style, with written captions).

(c)   Examine a whole range of books from 'precious' ones with beautiful bindings to paper-backs. Discuss reasons for different bindings: wearing qualities, value of content, enjoyment of appearance and 'feel', availability (i.e. cheapness and value for money). The Bible may well be one which appears in every category. Find out how books are bound. *Bind* a shabby but useful book according to taste.

(d)   Writers with something special to say: St Luke writes about Jesus and later St Paul—Luke 1. 1–4; Acts 1. Special interests of St Luke shown by the incidents he chooses to include, e.g. the healings of outcasts, especially women—find examples of these.
Make a wall newspaper of some of these incidents. Either use illustrations of the original happenings, or modern equivalents from newspapers and missionary magazines (e.g. pictures of hospital wards, rescue operations, women ministering to those in need, outcasts, etc.).
Look up St Luke's account of the Last Supper and compare with words of consecration in the Prayer Book.

(e)   Luke the Biographer; all we know of St Paul's life, apart from the Epistles, and work is recorded by St Luke. Look at the 'we' passages in Acts. St Luke was a keen observer who accompanied Paul and carefully recorded events. 'Interview' St Luke as a newspaper reporter, asking for his impressions of St Paul as a man, and write a newspaper article.

2.   LUKE THE HEALER

(a)   Investigate the work of a general practitioner today (a doctor in the parish might help). He visits and treats people's diseases, takes surgery, prescribes medicine, etc. *Make* a plan of a doctor's day. (Younger children dramatise.)
He has people to help him—hospitals, specialists, nurses, chemists. Apparatus to help—heart and kidney machines, etc. drugs and vaccines, stethoscope and thermometer.

(b)   Investigate the rapid progress of medicine and surgery in the present century. (Older children might discover some of the crude remedies and forms of surgery in past centuries.)

(c) Healing in St Luke's day was not as crude as in the Middle Ages. The Greeks were advanced in surgery and medicine, as archaeologists' discoveries of surgical instruments prove. St Luke was a Greek (possibly from Macedonia—Acts 16. 9, 10) who would probably be able to use such instruments. Paul refers to him as 'the beloved physician' (Col. 4. 14).

(d) Read to the children the Hippocratic Oath. The Greek physician named Hippocrates was the 'father' of modern medicine and the oath to save life rather than destroy it is attributed to him. This oath is taken by all doctors today.

St Luke would probably have taken this oath and would find that it agreed completely with his Christian faith—see St. John 10. v. 10.

(e) St Luke shows his interest in healing in his Gospel. He records many instances of healing specific diseases, some of which are not recorded in other gospels (see below).

Look up: Luke 13. 10–17 Crippled woman
14. 1–6 Man with dropsy
17. 11–19 Ten lepers (Note that they were to follow the proper procedure of being certified as 'clean')
22. 50–53 Malchus (compare St John 18. 10. Only Luke mentions that Jesus healed him)
7. 11–17 Widow's son at Nain

(f) Luke accompanied St Paul—perhaps as his physician; Paul, not a robust man, had a particular ailment (2 Cor. 10. 10). Luke joined him on his second missionary journey. (Acts 16. 11, 12.)

3. LUKE THE ARTIST

(There is a strong tradition that St Luke was also an artist and that a likeness of Christ painted on the walls of the catacombs in Rome was painted by him. This was the first 'icon' or holy picture venerated by Christians.)

(a) Get children to bring several photographs of themselves and compare them—some good, some not so good, but all recognisable? Discuss what makes a photograph or portrait recognisable. Features? colouring? figure? etc. Altogether these produce a likeness.

Get as many children as possible to paint or draw a portrait of one child and compare. (Artistic skill is not important here; careful observation *is*.)

(*b*) Look at portraits by great artists. (Medici Society postcards and art magazines or art folios in 'large book' sections of public libraries will offer examples.) Older children may be encouraged to look for other aspects of portraiture besides accurate reproduction of features, e.g. attitudes, expressions, character, etc.

(*c*) Discuss character, expression, features and possible physique of Jesus. Let children then *paint their own* portrait of him. After these have been looked at and discussed, look at some of the great artists' pictures of Jesus, including modern pictures. Are those *portraits* or artists' pictures? First portrait of Jesus attributed to St Luke, painted on walls of catacombs. Likeness of St Paul which may also be by him is in catacombs (reproduced in *Spreading the Gospel* by Bernard Youngman, pp. 24 and 55).

Discuss: How would St Luke know what Jesus was like? He may never have met him as he (Luke) possibly lived in Antioch.

Summing up

Note that we learn most about St Luke from the things he was *able to do*. There are no written accounts of him. We learn about him from his written 'portrait' of Jesus (more important than the painted one) and his written 'portrait' of Paul, and also from the fact that Paul called him the 'beloved physician' (Col. 4, 14). Get children to write or describe Luke's character from this evidence.

Notes on using the course

There is very little information about St Luke from sources outside the New Testament, but it is generally supposed that he was a well educated Greek (a Gentile) who lived at Antioch where, presumably, he came under the influence of St Paul. He has also been identified by some with the 'man of Macedonia', as the 'we' passages in the Acts begin from that moment. The introductions to the Gospel of St Luke and the Acts of the Apostles in *The Concise Bible Commentary* by Lowther Clarke give some details. Whether or not he was actually a painter, he was certainly a literary artist and without his portraiture of Jesus and Paul the Christian Church would be infinitely poorer.

Books for teachers

The Concise Bible Commentary, by Lowther Clarke (SPCK).
New World, Book III and IV, by Alan Dale (OUP), also for children.
Spreading the Gospel. (Background to the Bible, Book 4), by Bernard Youngman (Hulton).

Pictures

Art Folios from public libraries will afford a variety of portraits.
' Portraits ' of Jesus might include Fra Angelico's *Transfiguration* (SPCK *Christian Year* pictures); Michelangelo's *Last Judgement* (in the Sistine Chapel); El Greco's *Agony in the Garden* (SPCK); Graham Sutherland's *Crucifixion* (in *New World*) and *Christ in Majesty* (in Coventry Cathedral).

Art books containing large reproductions of these pictures can be obtained through the public library.

LIGHT

A family service by Edward Jacson, suitable for November 5

Reading: Genesis 1. 1–5, as introduction to service.
Hymn: ' Praise to the Holiest ' (A & M 172).
Reading: Matthew 17. 1–8: the Transfiguration of Jesus.
Hymn: ' Christ whose glory fills the skies ' (A & M 7).

Address

' To understand the importance of light we need first of all to be in the dark, so I am going to ask the Verger, Mr R, to put the lights out.

(Lights out)

Now will you shut your eyes so you are quite in the dark?

It's rather frightening. We don't know where we are. Mind you don't fall off your seats!

Now feel around you and discover what is in front of you, behind, on either side. Now open your eyes. It is still rather gloomy, but there is some light. It comes from the sun, even though the sun is behind the dark clouds today.

Peter is now going to light two candles. Candlelight is a soft, warm light. Jane's got a torch here. It runs off batteries and is a useful light, especially at this time of the year when the days are so short.

Now I'm going to light a firework. I expect you've been enjoying fireworks earlier this week. Fireworks are fun. They have coloured lights and some go flash and bang. This one won't go bang. It's just a pretty light. Bonfires are warm, red, glowing lights. People have lit bonfires long before Guy Fawkes. I expect you have heard stories of explorers in the snow lighting fires to keep the wolves away and stop themselves from freezing to death.

We still haven't got much light in here. It's rather gloomy, so I'm going to ask Mr R to put on the electric lights.

(Nave lights on)

Yes, you look happier now and it seems much gayer in here. It is the same at home, isn't it? It would be very dull in the evening at

159

home without electric light. Electric light is also used in film studios and gives us our TV programmes and films at the cinema. What other uses are there for light?'

Draw out from children such things as:
Traffic lights
Brake and indicator lights on cars
Signalling lamps
Navigation lights on ships, etc.

Summarise briefly and draw attention to our need to thank God for light—one of his greatest gifts to us.
'Now we are going to thank God for light.'

Distribute tapers. Position two people either side of chancel arch to give lights from candles they hold. Ask everyone to find Hymn 573 and make their way, following priest, into chancel and sanctuary (still dark) with lighted tapers for prayer. After each line of prayer, people say 'Thank you, God, for light.'

Prayer:
The sun shines, giving light to the world by day:
Thank you, God, for light.
The moon reflects its light at night:
The stars shine at night:
A candle gives a soft warm light:
Fireworks are bright and exciting lights. Sometimes they flash and bang:
A bonfire gives a red, hot light:
An electric torch is a useful light:
Electric light makes our homes bright and gay:
Electric light at the cinema and theatre and on TV helps people to entertain us:
Traffic lights warn drivers when to stop and when it is safe to go:
Brake lights and flashing lights on cars tell other drivers what we are about to do:
Street lamps light our way:
God led his ancient people Israel with a pillar of fire and appeared on Mount Sinai to Moses in flashing light:
Jesus was transfigured in light:
He said, 'I am the Light of the world':
He has promised to make all who follow him Sons of Light:
In the beginning God said 'Let there be light' and there was light:
Thank you, God, for light.

Hymn: ' All things bright and beautiful ' (A & M 573).

Prayer:

Lighten our darkness we beseech thee, O Lord, and keep us from all dangers that may hurt us, this day and always, for Jesus Christ's sake. Amen.

The Blessing

NB *Either* put chancel lights on after Blessing and ask people to blow out tapers *or* ask them to leave quietly, putting tapers out as they reach the light part of the church. *Don't* plunge everyone into darkness in the chancel and sanctuary.

Remember before the service to have the children with their candles and torch properly briefed and be sure that the verger knows his cues !

Remember also the danger of fire, and beware of stray sparks. Use an ' indoor ' firework. It would be good if this service could be followed by a parish bonfire and firework party in the evening, complete with hot potatoes, treacle toffee and (if you live in the North) parkin.

STIRRING IT UP!

An idea for the Sunday before Advent family service, involving audience participation, by Rodney J. Pope

You will need: The ingredients for making a simple cake.

Today I thought that we would take the opportunity of making a cake. (*If there is time, ask the children to help you weigh and measure. If not:*) I expect that you can see that I have got the right ingredients here, I weighed them out before I came so that there would be no mistakes. This is a quick-mix cake, so all we have to do now that I have put the ingredients in the mixing bowl is to give it a good stir. Is there anyone here who would like to help me?

I expect that many of your mums are now beginning to make their Christmas puddings and maybe you help to stir up the mixture. Anyway there we are—our cake is all ready for the oven. Next Sunday I will bring it to Church so that you can all see how it turned out.

You may wonder why I am talking about making cakes and puddings. Well, while the official title of this Sunday is, ' The next before Advent ' we sometimes call it, ' Stir-up Sunday '. Do you know why? If you have a Prayer Book in front of you, look at today's Collect (Trinity 25). Do you see how it begins? . . . ' Stir up, we beseech . . .' That is why today is called Stir-up Sunday.

It reminds us that next Sunday is the beginning of a new Church year and so it is time for new resolutions about our Christian life. Perhaps we have become a little slack and careless with our prayers or our Bible reading or our worship. Perhaps our love and friendship for Jesus is not as real and vital as it used to be. It's time to ask him that we may be stirred up—we may find new life and new vitality.

Remember the cake which we have just prepared. It would not have been much of a cake unless it was very thoroughly stirred. The ingredients were all very good and desirable but what was absolutely essential was that they should be stirred up! We probably have many good ingredients in us, we are probably also full of good intentions—but the important thing is that they should be given a good stir.

Secret history of Stir Up Sunday

From Mr Neville Edwards

Sir, — How odd that Canon Holbrooke-Jones should regard the festival of Christ the King as "creeping Romanism" while disregarding the fact that the Prayer Book collect for Trinity 25 is itself a translation of the collect in the Sarum Missal, the original being in the Sacramentory of St Gregory (Letters, 3 December).

However, his choice of the word "creeping" is very apt, as the feast of Christ the King was instituted in the Roman Catholic Church in 1925.

NEVILLE EDWARDS
8 Queensway, Roydon, Diss
Norfolk IP22 3QT

LETTERS to the Editor should be exclusive to the *Church Times*.

Michael Manktelow

JOHN MOORMAN: Anglican, Franciscan, independent

Canterbury Press £12.99
(1-85311-310-7)

"I AM the only bishop on the bench who can milk a cow by hand," John Moorman proudly remarked to me on one of his visits to Chichester Theological College. Visits by one's predecessors are not always easy, but he was my favourite guest, charming, erudite, original.

This admirable memoir

comfortable for wartime. For over two years he worked as a farm labourer. In 1946 his hero Bishop Bell invited him to be principal at Chichester, where he presented a "true and steady Anglicanism". When he became Bishop of Ripon in 1959, a Yorkshireman described him as "a dainty man" (he was small in stature), but Moorman insisted he was "every millimetre a bishop".

His scholarship was invaluable when he was senior Anglican observer at the Second Vatican Council, and a member of ARCIC. He never thought that admiring Rome meant despising Canterbury, and he

Unfortunately we have great difficulty in stirring ourselves. We need God's help, that is why we have this special prayer for today in which we ask God to do just that. Those of you who have a Prayer Book at home could perhaps make a point of using that prayer every day this week. If you do not have a prayer book or are too small to use grown-up prayers like that, you can still remember to ask God each day to give you a real stir.

(*Next Sunday, perhaps, you can all share the cake.*)

ADVENT IS EXCITING!

Sheila Longbottom and Irene Bickerdyke emphasise preparation for Christmas in a theme for 3s to 7s

Aim
In the weeks leading to Christmas we want to instil into the children of our threes to sevens group the spirit of excitement and wonder surrounding the birth of the Baby at Bethlehem.

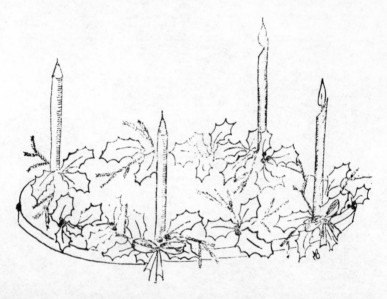

Advent ring and Advent calendar
These were used as the central points of our worship in the four Sundays of Advent. Each Sunday a candle was lit and another window of the calendar opened as part of the Christmas story was told. We used the Ladybird book *The Little Lord Jesus* with the story divided into four parts for the narration. This ceremony (done by different children each week) together with prayers and a hymn started Sunday school, and then we divided into handwork groups with a large choice of activities.

Advent ring

Materials used

Cake board, Plasticine, holly, greenery, four candles, white paint, glitter, green ribbon, pins.

Method

Roll Plasticine into a sausage, then bend into a circle about 2" smaller than the diameter of the cake board. Press into place on the board. Fix candles into Plasticine around the ring and fill spaces to cover Plasticine with holly and other greenery. Brush edges of holly leaves with white paint and sprinkle with glitter while it is still wet.

Tie green ribbon into four bows with tails and place one beneath each candle. Secure to Plasticine with a pin.

Advent calendar

Materials used

1 sheet wrapping paper or other large picture. We used a beautiful paper depicting a Nativity scene from a medieval manuscript.

Four Christmas cards showing:

1. Journey to Bethlehem (beware those showing Flight into Egypt!).
2. The Birth of Christ in the stable.
3. The Shepherds.
4. The Three Wise Men.

Gold foil. Two lengths of timber lathe approximately the width of the paper. Sheet of cardboard for a backing paper. Thin cord. Gold string.

Method

Decide where on the paper you wish the windows to be and draw round the Christmas card which will appear there. Cut round three sides of the rectangle about $\frac{1}{4}"$ inside the card edge. Place the sheet of wrapping paper on the cardboard and mark placings of cards, then glue them into position. Glue the top paper and the backing sheet together round the edges. Glue the wooden lathes to the top and bottom edges of the calendar. Secure hanging cord with two drawing pins. Cut out numerals one, two, three and four from gold foil and stick to appropriate window. Tie the windows into closed position with gold string.

Christmas cards

1. *Wrapping paper idea: materials used*

Wrapping paper, glue, glitter, thin card.

Method

Choose a wrapping paper which shows small figures or interesting motifs. Cut this out either very neatly or in irregular blobs, according to choice. Brush liberally with glue and place in centre of card, pressing the surplus glue to the edge of the picture. Dust with glitter, which will adhere to the surplus glue.

2. *Christmas Tree cards: materials used*

Thin card, crayons or paint, glitter.

Method

Cut card into shape of a Christmas tree. Colour, then decorate with glitter.

3. *Crib*

White cut-outs on black paper proved effective.

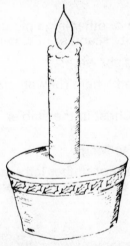

Christmas presents

1. *Christmas candle: materials used*

Toilet-roll middle, foil, margarine container, cotton wool.

2. *Table mats: materials used*

Beer mats, glue, wallpaper or wrapping paper, Christmas tape.

Method

Cover beer mats on both sides with wallpaper or wrapping paper. Let each child make six, then tie together with gay tape in a bow.

If the coverings have been cut out to the size of the mats before the lesson, this can be done by the youngest children.

3. Containers
Cover yoghourt or cream cartons with wallpaper, fabric, or Fablon. (N.B. use a rubber-based glue.) These make attractive containers for sweets, bath salts, etc.

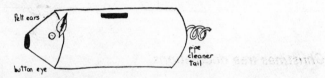

4. Money box: materials used
Squeezy bottle, crêpe paper, pipe cleaner, buttons.

5. Bookmark
Cut rectangle of felt $1\frac{1}{2}"\times8"$. Fringe shorter edges. Decorate with felt bits, sequins, cotton, etc.

Suggested carols
' Away in a manger '
' The Rocking Carol '
' Once in royal David's city '
' The Birds' Carol ' (*Oxford Carol Book*)
' Jesus, good above all other '

Children's prayers
1. Thank you, God, for helping us to make plans for Christmas. May we remember, as we make our cards and decorations, that we have Christmas because your son Jesus was born in a stable at Bethlehem. Help us to love our babies at home.

2. Thank you, God, for our lovely Christmas food and presents. Thank you for fun in the snow. Thank you for the Christmas tree with its coloured lights. We love the crib in church and the carols we sing round it. Thank you, God, for Christmas.

3. Lord Jesus, please help me to be good. Remind me to say thank you to people when they give me Christmas presents, even if I don't like them. Let me help my Mummy and Daddy as you helped Mary and Joseph.

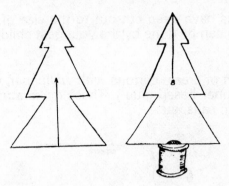

Christmas tree decorations

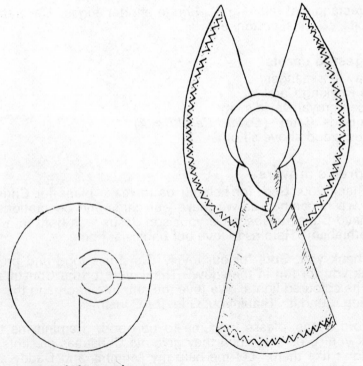

Christmas angel decorations

List of books

There are some wonderful books about the Christmas story. Look around the bookshops. Here are a few suggestions:

The Christmas Book, by Dick Bruna. (Methuen)

The Little Lord Jesus, Baby Jesus, and *Christmas Customs* (for reference), all Ladybird Books.

Eight Days to Christmas, by Geraldine Kaye. A Nipper Book. (Macmillan)

The Magic Christmas Tree, by Lee Kingman. (OUP)

The one we were waiting for, by Pamela Egan. A Rainbow Book (CIO)

Jesus is born, A Sunflower Book. (CIO)

Where is the King? A Sunflower Book (CIO)

THE POWER OF LIGHT

A theme full of possibilities
for exploration during Advent

For four days the children of Byfield, near Daventry, explored the theme of ' Light ' in a holiday course. One highspot of their week was the construction of an illuminated village, with street lighting and a floodlit church, construction plans for which are included in this article.

The ' textbook ' used by the Vicar, the Rev. Andrew Freer, who designed and ran the course with the aid of three teenage helpers, was *Light, Mirrors and Lenses*, a Ladybird Junior Science book. He divided the work into four sections; in each, he gave a simple lecture-demonstration and joined in a practical exploration with the children. The sections were:

1. Sight How the eye works, demonstrated by a model ' eye ' made from a goldfish bowl; things we enjoy seeing; ' eyes ' for the blind—in which the children found out about the training of guide dogs and practised using Braille.

2. Things that give and reflect light The light of the sun and stars; lamps through the ages (this section included a display of antique lamps); the moon; reflectors such as cat's-eyes, safety armbands and mirrors.

3. Light and colour The spectrum, prisms, what makes a rainbow, the kaleidoscope.

4. Light can play tricks Some optical illusions, such as refraction and the ' ghost candle ' trick in the Ladybird book.

The older children (ages in the group ranged from 5 to 11) worked on the model village, wiring it with the Vicar's help, assembling and colouring the houses and church and making the street lights. Trees were made from paper, and an avenue of ' yews ' up to the church door from tufts of a brush, coloured green. Younger children laid out and coloured the gardens of each house. A lighthouse was also made, with meccano ' works ' which rotated the light, and other models included a kaleidoscope, spectrum discs and the ' ghost candle '. Meanwhile the youngest children

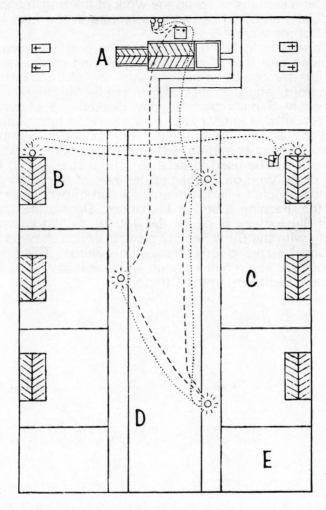

A Church has square tower, chancel made from one ' house ', nave from larger ' house ', both with roofs adapted to fix inside walls, to allow for parapet.   Nave conceals a 6 volt battery feeding two 2·5v. bulbs in series and a separate 5v. bulb for street lights.   Churchyard laid out and coloured.   All wiring goes under base board.

B Houses made and coloured by older children from pattern on page 173.   Floodlights work from a two cell cycle battery concealed under house opposite, feeding two lens bulbs in parallel.

C Gardens drawn and coloured by younger children.

D Road painted black with pavements for street-lamps.

E Green ' grass ' with paper trees.

drew or coloured scenes from Christ's life, illustrations of the parables, and pictures showing the work of the British and Foreign Bible Society, all of which were to feature in the final ' drawing together ' of the work.

Each afternoon included a short singing practice, accompanied by the organ and four of the children playing recorders. Hymns chosen for the course were ' Awake, my soul ', ' Thou whose almighty word,' and two specially written by Mr Freer.

The Family Service that Sunday marked the climax of the course. Stage by stage Mr Freer re-capped the four sections, and the children helped to build up in the church an exhibition of the work they had done, ending with the section on ' tricks '. From ' light which can be used to deceive ', the theme moved to Christ the True Light, who gave sight to the eyes of the blind and who enlightened people's minds through the sort of person he was and through the teaching found in his stories. During this last stage, panels of illustrations done by the youngest children were built up, ending with the Bible Society pictures which showed how the light of Christ is spread today through his words. This first part of the service took about half an hour, and was followed by the Holy Communion, beginning at the Offertory.

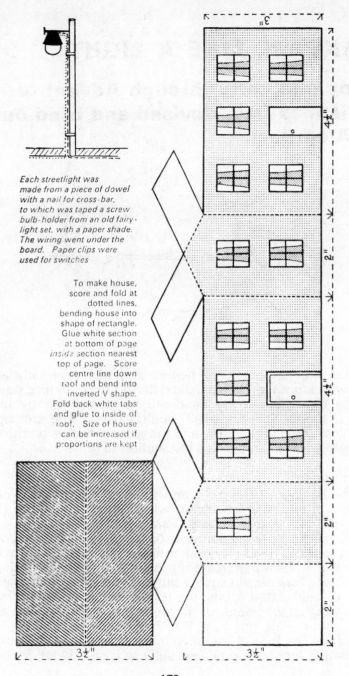

Each streetlight was made from a piece of dowel with a nail for cross-bar, to which was taped a screw bulb-holder from an old fairy-light set, with a paper shade. The wiring went under the board. Paper clips were used for switches

To make house, score and fold at dotted lines, bending house into shape of rectangle. Glue white section at bottom of page *inside* section nearest top of page. Score centre line down roof and bend into inverted V shape. Fold back white tabs and glue to inside of roof. Size of house can be increased if proportions are kept

3"

4½"

2"

4½"

2"

2"

3½"

3½"

MAKE ME LIKE A LIGHT . . .

A topic to carry through Advent to Christmas Day, devised and tried out by Alan Beck

Children are fascinated by flames and fire, especially as many children seldom see a live or naked flame today. In fact, power cuts can be fun—bathing by candle light, homework by hurricane lantern, supper lit by a small paraffin lamp. The soft light, the unfamiliar angle of the light, and the great shadows on the wall . . .

At Advent we can put this fascination to good use.

Introduction

Tell the parable of the wise and foolish virgins and explain the customs of an Eastern wedding which underlie it. (See Ladybird series 649, No. 2, *Life in New Testament Times.*)

Describe the ordinary domestic oil lamp of Our Lord's day, which was made from dried clay, rather like a small flat teapot without a lid, or like a small flat cream jug, with a short wick in the spout. The secret of success in such a simple lamp is the fuel. If you used petrol or methylated spirits, the whole lot would go up in flames when a match was applied. If you used paraffin, it would smoke badly. But in Palestine then, they had none of these fuels, only oil made from the fruit of the olive tree. This was quite plentiful, so they used it for cooking oil (we still use it on salads), for ointment and to clean the skin. We still have palm and olive oil in Palmolive soap. (A bottle of olive oil could be examined and children asked to find out if their mother has some at home in the larder.)

This oil makes a good fuel for a simple lamp because it does not smoke readily and will not burn unless vaporised by a wick, so it cannot be set alight accidentally. The lamp used in Jesus' time was therefore simple and easy to make, safe to use—but there was one draw-back: you couldn't adjust the wick, so the height of the flame depended on how much oil there was in the lamp and how far the oil had to travel up the wick. To keep a steady bright flame, you had to keep topping it up regularly. So the bridesmaids had to keep checking their lamps and putting in a bit more oil to keep the flame from burning low, when it could easily have blown out.

Advent is all about getting ready for when Christ comes at Christmas. We are to get ready by taking more care to *be* ready now, for although we know the date of Christmas Day, the days fly by and there is so much to prepare for Christmas that this, the most important part of getting ready for Christmas, can be overlooked. Christmas can come and find us like the foolish bridesmaids, unready—tired, cross, over-excited and thinking far too much about ourselves. So right from the beginning of Advent we take more care with our Sunday worship and our daily prayers. Some Christians light a candle when they pray. (Talk about, and if possible go and light, the altar candles.) We can think of our prayers as like a lamp burning to welcome Jesus. We will need to 'top up' this lamp regularly with prayers night and morning to keep it burning brightly.

Things to do

1. Demonstrate how olive oil burns by putting a little into a shallow dish such as an enamel plate. Light a match and dowse it in the oil. (*Don't* demonstrate what would happen if it were petrol!) Put a short length, about $1\frac{1}{2}$" of cotton string on the edge of the plate with the end dipping into the oil. Light the wick and vary the height of the flame by tipping oil towards the flame and away from it.

2. If possible, make simple lamps with clay, dry them off during the week, fill and light on Advent 2, top up and light again on Advent 3 and 4. If clay is not available. Polyfilla might be possible. Plasticine could be used, but the lamp couldn't be filled and lit. The shape is very simple: roll the clay out flat, shape it into a deep saucer, bend the sides upwards and pinch together to form a spout for the wick. Use cotton string for the wick.

3. Let children make a card with an Easter lamp—its easy outline can be drawn, cut from gummed paper or filled in with mosaic. Tinies could colour a ready-made card.

Compose a prayer and add it below the lamp, or you could use:

> Lord,
> Make me
> like a light
> shining bright,
> to welcome you
> at Christmas.

To be taken home and used daily in Advent.

4. Hymns and songs—anything from ' Jesus bids us shine ' to ' This little light of mine ' and the first verse of ' Christ, whose glory fills the skies '.

On Advent 4 or Christmas Eve.

It is nearly Christmas but not quite! By now, perhaps, the crib is in church but not the figures yet. Tell the story of Mary and Joseph arriving at Bethlehem. It was growing dark. They could find no shelter until someone lent them a stable. At least it was warmer than outdoors and dry. It was obvious that Mary's baby would soon be born. She needed essentials such as a bowl of water. Probably all she had with her were the baby clothes. Above all they needed a lamp. But the town was crowded out and everyone wanted lamps. There were not enough to go round. Likewise bowls, jugs. Did someone go to bed that night in the dark and without a wash so that they could lend their lamp, etc., to Mary? Think of the friendly soft light from the lamp burning in the corner, well away from draughts and on a stand or in a niche in the wall so that the animals would not knock it over. Think of it burning all through the time of waiting, ready to give light when Jesus was born. Our prayers through Advent and our continuing prayers now are like that light.

But soon Christ the Light of the world will be born! The church will be full of light, the brightest white frontal, all the lights switched on, every candle lit. We will come and share that light. When you come on Christmas Day, every one of you will receive a candle. We will all light our candle from the big candle which will be burning by the crib to represent Christ the Light of the world. We will stand round the crib and sing our carols by the light of our candles. Then we will take our candle home to set it in pride of place on the Christmas table, to stand for Christ who has come into our homes and hearts.

Hymn for Christmas Eve: ' O little town of Bethlehem ' first verse only.

But we mustn't drip wax everywhere, so the candles must have holders. (Issue previously prepared squares of card with the centre marked or cut so that the candle can be pushed through. The corners of the card can be bent down to make a candle stand, or the card can be pushed well up the candle to make a collar, the candle being held below the collar. The cards should be decorated —at home if necessary—as brightly as possible e.g. with glitter, and brought back on Christmas Day, when some spare ones should also be available.)

Teachers who wish to explore the whole theme of ' Light and Darkness ' in greater depth, or to add other resources to the ideas given here, are referred to the course of that name in *All Together Two* (CIO).

CAROLS FOR ADVENT— OR FOR EPIPHANY?

Paul Faunch expresses the dissatisfaction felt by many at the conventional carol service

The real time to start planning next year's carol service is, of course on the morning after this year's. Though, strictly speaking, we are not entirely correct when we think of ' the ' Carol Service as being concerned only with Christmas. No organisers of a service of lessons and carols should start work on their programme without first reading (at least) the prefaces to the *English Hymnal*, the *Oxford Book of Carols*, and, for good measure, Erik Routley's book *The English Carol* (Herbert Jenkins, now out of print), to discover more about the place of carols in the Church.

For all that, there will be many of us who, living from hand to mouth, will start to draw up a programme for a ' Christmas Carol Service ' to be performed during the opening days of December, based on the nine lections used at King's College, Cambridge, on Christmas Eve, interspersed with such items from (say) *Singing Together* as we think that our class or choir can perform. All this programmising, to be done two or three days before the service is due to take place! The great popularity of the King's College service is demonstrated by the way every school and almost every club we know, wants to have its own ' carol service ' based on the King's programme.

In the parish where the present writer served, there were six different schools each of which, every Advent, had its own service of nine lessons in the parish church. The Sunday school had its own service, and then the church choir another one. The six school services all planned to have the Christmas Day collect read, and to march out at the conclusion singing 'Glory to the new-born king'— all this, of course, two or three weeks before Christmas. By the time of the Christmas Eve service, when the nurses from the hospital came in singing 'The first Nowell' (really an *Epiphany* song) many people were quite ' tired of Christmas '!

In planning the school or Sunday school carol festival service, are we really committed to *nine* lessons? But what is more basic,

I think, is the question ' Are we committed to sing the whole story before Christmas has really begun?' I would like to suggest that a school service in Advent might more realistically be described as a ' Service in preparation for Christmas '. The lessons would mostly trace the Old Testament ' preparations ' for the first Christmas, the Annunciation, and then, as the last ' gospel ', why not use *Hebrews* 1—probably verses 1–3 would be sufficient. The final collect could be that for Christmas Eve in the 1928 Prayer Book, or something of the kind.

In such a service, the opening hymn might well be ' O come, O come, Emmanuel '. (Choirmasters please see that it is sung in unison, without organ pedals, except for the occasional refrain, and with a free speech-rhythm. The more recent editions of hymn-books are usually better in this matter than the older ones.)

The great Advent Antiphons given in the English Hymnal might well be used, even if only *read* as versicle and response after each lesson. (Counsel of perfection for a grammar school or adult service.)

The last hymn could be 'While shepherds watch' or' Angels from the realms of glory '.

I would strongly recommend that there be no crib set up for this service though, to add some visual interest, singers might come in with lighted lanterns or tapers.

The Christmas story from St Luke is now ' in the wings ' ready for Christmas: and we still have the wise men (up our sleeves, so to speak) for January, and, for good measure, the keeping up of the old festival of Candlemas on February 2nd.

The Sunday after Epiphany is the time for the whole Christmas story to be set forth in its full glory. Not until Epiphany should any hymn or carol be sung where the wise men are mentioned.

But once again, the festival of carols in Epiphany-tide need not be just a repetition of the King's College service. Most of our imitations of that service are, anyway travesties of it from the artistic point of view.

I would recommend an ' extension ' of Evensong. The following programme, which I have used for ten years or so, works well on a Sunday evening:

The Bidding (as used at King's College, but with the words ' This Epiphany ' instead of ' Christmastide ').

All remain standing for the opening versicles and responses of Evensong.

Office hymn ' Behold the great Creator makes himself a house of clay ' or ' Of the Father's love begotten '.

Psalm: 45

Lesson I: Genesis 3. 1–15

Carol:

Lesson II: Numbers 24. 15–18.

Carol:

Lesson III: Isaiah 9. 2, 6, 7 (omit the comma between ' Wonderful ' and ' Counsellor ').

Hymn: ' The people that in darkness sat.'

Lesson IV: The Annunciation: Luke 1. 26–37.

Magnificat:

Lesson V: Matthew 1. 18 to end.

Lesson VI: Luke 2. 1–20

Carol: ' While shepherds watched.'
(A group of carols if desired.)

Lesson VII: Matthew 2. 1–12.
An Epiphany carol or carols.

Nunc Dimittis

Creed

Lesser Litany, Lord's Prayer, suffrages, collects of Evensong.

Hymn: (say) ' O worship the Lord in the beauty of holiness ' and collection.

General Thanksgiving.

Grace.

Hymn: ' The first Nowell ' (or similar).

Blessing.

For good measure, either of these services can include some visual material. The Advent service can commence with the reader and singers at the back of the church. Each lesson is read at a pillar or stage nearer to the front, the singers processing forward to the next ' station ' as they sing, the last lesson being read from the lectern in front, or even from the sanctuary, according to the convenience of all concerned. This looks splendid in a gothic-style building lit by candles, with the lectors accompanied by ' taperers '. For the Epiphany service, one could omit the first two lessons on our list. Isaiah could be read from the back of the church, or from the pulpit. The other lessons could be read ' dramatically ' by several readers. Meanwhile, the stories can be mimed. In East Donyland church, we finish up with ' O come all ye faithful '. During the verse ' Sing choirs of angels,' children come in with percussion band instruments, and dance round the font, in time to the hymn. By the end of it, they are at the crib before the altar. ' Gabriel ' then gives them each a lighted candle which is carried solemnly out of church to an organ voluntary.

A TREE FOR EPIPHANY

Alan Beck suggests a topic for the 'dead days' after Christmas

By the time we met for our monthly Family Service on the first Sunday after the Epiphany, my Sunday school teachers were very glad that it was 'church Sunday' and not Sunday school, as Christmas by then seemed well and truly over. The children had started practising carols half way through last term, and now in two days' time it would be next term! Dustbins overflowed with discarded paper decorations; forlorn Christmas trees stood beside them. If we talked about the wise men, how could we fail to give the impression that church and Sunday school were out of date and out of touch?

So we began by asking 'were the wise men too late?' Actually they could have been as much as two years late (Matt 2. 16) but of course they were not really too late, for Jesus was still on earth to be visited. He hadn't gone back to heaven as soon as Christmas was over. He continued to live and grow and probably was no longer in the stable when they arrived but a little boy growing up in a family home. The Christmas story goes on after Christmas to Jesus' boyhood, manhood and ministry.

Likewise the Christmas story must go on for us too. At Christmas something was born (or re-born) in us—our love for Jesus. We sang (in 'Away in a manger') 'I love thee, Lord Jesus'. As Jesus grew, so our love should grow. How shall we remember this? On Christmas Eve and Christmas Day we made a picture of a Christmas tree. It was *green*, to stand for all that lives and grows.

At home you had a tree. If it was artificial it looked very pretty, but once Christmas was over, you packed it away until next Christmas. When you take it out of the cupboard next time it will not be any taller. Some people's Christmas is artificial. It looks pretty but it lacks real life, i.e. love for Jesus.

Perhaps you had a real tree, but one without any proper roots. It looked as if it were alive, but soon it began to drop its needles. Now it is clearly dead and must be thrown away. Jesus is sad if our love for him is like that—no roots and soon dead!

Perhaps you had a real little living tree with roots and were fortunate enough to have somewhere outside where you could

182

plant it after Christmas. Now it stands in the garden, looking rather ordinary without its decorations, but it is still green and we hope that it will take root and grow to remind you throughout the year that our love for Jesus should live and grow.

So to the visual aid! Every child was given a sheet of paper—we used old duplicating paper, 13"×8". Old Christmas Service sheets would do well. Ideally, green paper should be used. The speaker can use a double page of newspaper. Roll the paper into a tube (in our case 8" high), flatten the top and tear down the tube about 2". Push back into tube shape, squash the other way and tear again to make four bits sticking up. Bend these outwards to resemble a palm tree. Hold innermost ' branch ' and pull gently upwards allowing it to twist round as you do so. The result should be a tree which grows. You may know this as a party trick but not have thought of it in terms of visual aids.

When you have a tree that is beginning to grow, you need a ladder to help you to look after it, prune the branches, spray against insects, and so on, and also to help with fruit-picking, if it's a fruit tree, or decorating, if it's a Christmas tree. This can be linked with the aids we have to help our love for Jesus to grow—his words, his friends, his Church—and another visual aid can be made from rolled paper, following the pattern given on the next page.

TREE

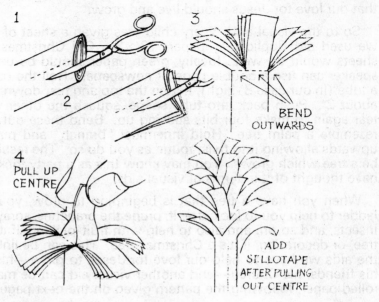

1

2

3

BEND OUTWARDS

4
PULL UP CENTRE

ADD SELLOTAPE AFTER PULLING OUT CENTRE

LADDER

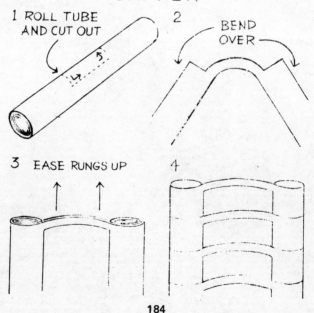

1 **ROLL TUBE AND CUT OUT**

2 **BEND OVER**

3 **EASE RUNGS UP**

4

184